Tiomnaím an leabhar seo do Mham

© Rialtas na hÉireann, 1993
Athchló, 1997

© Foras na Gaeilge, 2002
Athchló, 2002, 2005

ISBN 1-85791-079-6

Criterion Press Teo. a chlóbhuail in Éirinn.

Le fáil ar an bpost uathu seo:

An Siopa Leabhar,   *nó*   An Ceathrú Póilí,
6 Sráid Fhearchair,   Cultúrlann·Mac Adam–Ó Fiaich,
Baile Átha Cliath 2.   216 Bóthar na bhFál,
ansiopaleabhar@eircom.net   Béal Feirste BT12 6AH.
                                   leabhair@an4poili.com

Orduithe ó leabhardhíoltóirí chuig:
Áis,
31 Sráid na bhFíníní,
Baile Átha Cliath 2.
eolas@forasnagaeilge.ie

An Gúm, 24-27 Sráid Fhreidric Thuaidh, Baile Átha Cliath 1

LÁ le MAMÓ

Mary Arrigan
a scríobh agus a mhaisigh

Oiriúnach do pháistí ó 4 – 6 bliana d'aois

 **AN GÚM**
Baile Átha Cliath

Tá Mamó ag dúiseacht.
'Dia duit ar maidin, a Ghrian,' arsa
Mamó.
'Beidh bricfeasta agam anois,' ar sise.

Tá na héadaí ar an líne ag rince.
Tá Mamó ag rince ar an líne.

Tá Mamó ag rothaíocht faoin tuath.
'Fág an bealach!' arsa Mamó.

'Tá Mamó ag éisteacht leis an éan.
'Is breá liom do cheol, a Éinín,' arsa
Mamó.

'Tá mé ag léim thar an ngeata,' arsa Mamó.
Tá na hainmhithe ag féachaint uirthi.

'Is maith liom a bheith ag rith,' arsa an garsún.

'Tá deifir ormsa, a gharsúin,' arsa Mamó.

Nach álainn iad na balúin.
'Tá mé ag eitilt. Tá mé ag eitilt!' arsa Mamó.

Tá an ghealach ina suí.
'Oíche mhaith, a Ghealach,' arsa
Mamó. 'Tá mé ag dul abhaile.'

Tá Mamó ag glanadh a cuid fiacla.
Scuab agus taos fiacla atá aici.

Tá Mamó ina codladh.
Tá tuirse uirthi tar éis an lae.

Buses Restored
2000

Buses Restored
2000

Compiled by the
National Association of Road Transport Museums

Ian Allan PUBLISHING

Front Cover: Former East Kent AEC Regent V/Park Royal 6801 FN dating from 1963 is seen at Whitfield in July 1999. *Philip Lamb*

Back Cover: Former Lincoln City Transport 89 (RFE 416) is a 1961 Roe-bodied Leyland PD2, now in the care of the Lincolnshire Road Transport Museum. *Philip Lamb*

Half-title: A recently-completed restoration project is one-time Colchester No 4 (OHK 432), a Roberts-bodied Daimler CVD6 of 1949. Now kept at the Lincolnshire Road Transport Museum, the bus is seen during 1999. *Philip Lamb*

Title Page: Three Fleetlines in the care of the Birmingham & Midland Motor Omnibus Trust, Wythall; from left to right are former Birmingham Daimlers 3474 (BON 474C) and 3880 (NOV 880G) and former West Midlands Leyland 6311 (KON 311P). *Stephen Morris*

Below: AHF 850 is a Metro-Cammell-bodied Leyland PD2 new as Wallasey 54 in 1951, and is now housed at the Wirral Transport Museum in Birkenhead. *Philip Lamb*

First published 2000

ISBN 0 7110 2747 1

Published by Ian Allan Publishing

an imprint of Ian Allan Publishing Ltd, Terminal House, Shepperton, Surrey TW17 8AS.
Printed by Ian Allan Printing Ltd, Riverdene Business Park, Hersham, Surrey KT12 4RG.

Code: 0004/B2

Every effort has been made in this book to provide accurate information; the Publishers accept no liability for any loss, damage or injury caused by error or inaccuracy in the data provided in *Buses Restored 2000*.

Contents

Useful addresses

NARTM, PO Box 5141, Burton-upon-Trent DE15 OZF.

The Transport Trust, 202 Lambeth Road, London SE1 7JW.

British Bus Preservation Group, 18 Greenriggs, Hedley Park, Stopsley, Luton LU2 9TQ.

The PSV Circle, 26 Ashville Grove, Halifax HX2 OPN.

Introduction

Welcome to the first edition of *Buses Restored*.

It is now over 40 years since the pioneers of bus preservation first took steps to save a small number of elderly buses from their fate in the scrapyard. Many of those involved in the early years are still active in the hobby and are connected with several of the projects described in this book.

In the late 1950s, preservation of all kinds of large transport relics was really in its infancy. Old cars had been retained for many years, but saving larger items such as railway locomotives, trams, boats and buses was considered to be a decidedly eccentric activity! Led by the successful examples of the Talyllyn and Ffestiniog railways in Wales and the first tram preservationists who came together at Crich in Derbyshire, enthusiasts were shown that it was quite feasible to club together and buy an old vehicle out of service.

Most of the vehicles saved lived in the corners of barns, or even out in the open, and inevitably a number suffered from the elements and faded from the scene. However, some buses were owned by those made of sterner stuff and, gradually, better accommodation was found and even purchased in some cases by the more visionary groups. These early successes included the Lincolnshire Vintage Vehicle Society, the London Bus Preservation Group and Colin Shears' West of England Transport Collection, all of whose current collections are listed in this book.

As nostalgia and looking back at the so-called 'golden days' of the past became popular, more buses and coaches were purchased and restored. Again, some fell by the wayside when major defects developed with the vehicle or when their owners' interests changed. The big reduction in regular service use of half-cab buses in most areas during the 1970s spurred more bus enthusiasts to dip into their pockets, saving a favourite old bus. This gave rise to today's good representation in preservation of buses dating from the 1950s and 1960s which were then being taken out of service.

Over the years, vehicle collections began to grow and amalgamate, giving greater stability and helping to provide a long-term future for the vehicles. Enthusiasts' groups realised that it might be possible to open museums, operated by volunteers, where the public could come and look at the vehicles from the past, and these ideas began to take root in several parts of the country. This movement helped to address the main problem faced by bus preservationists — where do you keep a large item such as a bus or coach?

The growing museums and collections, therefore, provided facilities to support individual efforts in the field. By pooling resources, money might be raised to rent or buy covered and secure premises. Skilled volunteers were able to offer help in restoration and to pass on those skills to others in the group. By opening to the public, revenue might be raised to help fund the upkeep of the project and its premises. Most important of all in the long term, those vehicles have been provided with a secure and sustainable home where they can be seen and used as an educational and cultural resource for the wider community. Bus museums can today be found in all parts of Britain and Ireland.

Not all collections of old buses are regularly open to the public. Some groups aspire to provide a formal display at some time in the future. Others prefer to concentrate their efforts on vehicle conservation and their vehicles can usually only be seen at some of the many rallies, running days and open days.

Although outside the scope of this present edition, there are many more preserved buses and coaches in private hands which are well looked after and which can often be seen on rally fields during the summer months. The British Bus Preservation Group provides a focus for these vehicles and is in the process of compiling a list of privately-owned vehicles — it is hoped to incorporate this information in a future edition of this book. In 1999 the PSV Circle also compiled a comprehensive list of

Above left: Three ex-London Transport prewar AEC Regals are seen in Staines. From left to right are Cobham Bus Museum's LPTB-bodied Green Line coach T504 (ELP 228) of 1938, the LT Museum's Duple-bodied Green Line coach T219 (GK 5486) of 1931 and Cobham's LGOC-bodied bus T31 (UU 6646) of 1929. *Stephen Morris*

Left: Another prewar Green Line coach, LPTB-bodied Leyland Tiger TF77 (FJJ 774) of 1939, is seen outside the London Transport Museum in Covent Garden. *Stephen Morris*

preserved buses and coaches. Contact details for these and other groups are given on page 5.

Bus services using historic vehicles from all sectors of the preservation world are a popular way of making the old buses and coaches come to life, and allow the public to experience just what it was like to travel on public transport in the past. Some elderly buses have even gained a new lease of life and are back in commercial use, often in connection with other tourist attractions. These services can re-create the experience of riding on buses from earlier generations, bringing back memories of the time when bus and coach travel was a normal part of life for the majority of people.

We hope that readers will use this book to explore the many excellent museums described and to learn about the everyday travel experiences which have changed for ever. Each museum has its own distinctive character and many also display other types of vehicle, from bicycles through cars to vans and lorries. Buses and coaches can frequently be seen at the rallies, running days and other events held throughout the year. *Preserved Bus*, *Classic Bus* and *Buses* magazines all carry details of forthcoming events and historic bus services, and are available from most high street newsagents.

When visiting the collections listed in this book, readers may like to make their journey using one of the modern generation of quiet, air-conditioned buses with easy-access low floors. Such vehicles are the descendants of those described in this book and show the next stages in the development of road passenger transport. One day even these buses will take their place alongside the Regents, Tigers, Arabs and others, in the museums and collections of the future.

Below: A selection of vehicles inside the Castle Point Transport Museum on Canvey Island. On the left, former Southend 244 (FOP 429) is a Daimler CWA6/Duple, new to Birmingham in 1944 and later operated by Eastern National; next to it is former Eastern National 2380 (WNO 478), an ECW-bodied Bristol KSW new to Westcliff-on-Sea in 1953. On the right is former Potteries L453 (NEH 453), a 1949 Leyland OPD2 with Northern Counties bodywork. Other vehicles visible include Bristol Lodekkas, AEC Regents and a now-departed Leyland Tiger coach. *Andy Izatt*

What is NARTM ?

The information in this book has been compiled from a database of preserved buses, trolleybuses and coaches generated by members of the National Association of Road Transport Museums (NARTM), which is an informal organisation of museums and collections, many of which are operated by volunteers. Other museums, such as the Transport Museum at Glasgow and the London Transport Museum are managed by full-time staff. This mix of museum types gives the opportunity to share ideas and experiences; the volunteers involved each bring their own professional skills to their projects, and best practices can then be shared by all the member museums and collections.

NARTM has been in existence for almost 20 years and now has around 30 member organisations, with more joining each year. The buses and coaches which form part of the NARTM collections are generally regarded as forming the nucleus of a National Collection of Buses and Coaches. Other important examples are in private hands outside the scope of NARTM and its members. For more information about NARTM, please contact the address given on page 5.

NARTM compiled the database in order to begin to quantify the size and scope of Public Service Vehicle preservation, and was prompted in this aim by the Transport Trust. The Trust is concerned that the items of transport interest which have been saved are also going to be secure in the long term, and that unique vehicles will not be lost when their owners are no longer able to look after them. By listing the vehicles which remain, it becomes much easier to assess the value of an individual vehicle which might be 'at risk', as it can be viewed in the context of the whole range of surviving similar vehicles.

Below: A standard ECW-bodied Bristol VR delivered in NBC poppy red in 1977, City of Oxford 476 (HUD 476S) received its operator's traditional livery in 1981 to mark 100 years of public transport in Oxford. The bus is now preserved in these colours at the Oxford Bus Museum, and is seen in Woodstock on the 1998 Bristol VR Running Day. *Philip Lamb*

Preserving and Restoring a Bus

How does one go about restoring a bus to its former glory? No two vehicles will have to go through exactly the same stages, but the process and areas needing attention are usually very similar.

The starting point is generally a vehicle in run-down condition — which is why it was taken out of use in the first place. If it could have been economically repaired in the commercial environment, its owner would have done just that. Other buses may be in an even worse state, having lingered in a scrapyard or even as a hen-house or storeshed for a number of years. Some may be no more than bare, rusty chassis, their bodywork having succumbed to the elements!

Restoration work can be roughly divided into three main areas: chassis and mechanical parts, body structure and interior. The last is the most familiar to the public and the enthusiast, as it is the area most visible day-to-day. However, with its upholstery and detailed trim, it can be the hardest area to restore so that it looks and feels right.

Hopefully, the body structure will be in better shape. This will depend on whether the bus has been kept undercover, and on whether it has a timber or a metal frame. Each type of frame has its own problems, but these are made worse by the

Below: Two vehicles awaiting restoration at the Birmingham & Midland Museum of Transport are one-time Sheffield 271 (OWE 271K), a 1972 Bristol VR/East Lancs, and former Midland Red 6015 (GHA 415D), a 'D12' class Daimler Fleetline/Alexander of 1966. Limited restoration work appears to have started on the latter, as the paintwork has been rubbed down and some panels have been replaced. *Stephen Morris*

Right: Former London Transport 1937 AEC Regent STL2377 undergoes restoration at Cobham Bus Museum. *Philip Lamb*

damp climate which will usually have penetrated to start the processes of rotting and corrosion. When working on this part of the bus it is important to ensure that the bus remains 'square' and is not allowed to go out of shape by the removal of too many parts at the same time.

The mechanical parts will often be the least familiar to the enthusiast, but they are really the most important as they are the major organs of the vehicle. The chassis itself is fairly unlikely to have suffered more than surface rust, and much of the work underneath the bus will consist of scraping off accumulated mud, oil and grease. The major areas needing attention are likely to be the brakes, oil seals and the exhaust system. The engine may well be in running order but, if it makes loud knocking-sounds or produces a lot of smoke, further work will be needed. The wiring system is another part of the vehicle which will often require replacement, especially if old types of cable were used — these will probably have perished, leaving the vehicle in a dangerous condition where short circuits (leading to fire) are likely.

It is important that each stage of the restoration be documented, ideally in a formal way. This will ensure that future generations know what has been done to the vehicle — where materials have been replaced with newer ones, and where additions such as direction indicators have been made for safety reasons. These latter details are what differentiate restoration from conservation, although both approaches produce fine-looking vehicles in near-original condition.

When the basic condition of the vehicle is satisfactory, coach-painting of the exterior can be attempted; this can be one of the most satisfying stages of bus restoration, or one of the most exasperating! When all is complete, the owner should report to the local Vehicle Inspectorate depot and, with any luck, come away with a Test Certificate.

Below: The final touches are applied to former Widnes Leyland National No 1 (RTC 645L) at St Helens Transport Museum. *Philip Lamb*

Right: The finished article! Restored to its former glory is former Walsall 116 (XDH 516G), one of the municipality's final, 1969 batch of short Daimler Fleetlines with Northern Counties bodywork. *Stephen Morris*

116
XDH 516G

TRANSPORT
BUS
STOP
MUSEUM

How to Use this Book

This book lists both formal museums and the more informal types of collection, and gives details of opening times, contact addresses and the facilities available, together with a list of the buses, trolleybuses and coaches on display. Many of the sites are open to the public on a regular basis. Admission fees vary and some are even free to visitors, although donations towards the upkeep of the collections are always welcome. Please be aware that the vehicles on display can vary from time to time. Not all museums are able to display their entire 'fleet', and some practice the regular rotation of exhibits for added interest. In addition, some of the vehicles may be in the process of restoration in a workshop off-site, and there is always the possibility that a bus may be on loan to another museum! Visitors wishing to see a particular vehicle should make enquiries prior to the visit.

Some collections are not normally available for public access. However, the owners usually welcome visitors and will arrange for viewing by prior application. In addition, many such groups do have open or public days from time to time. Contact addresses are provided in this book, and those wishing to visit a particular site are asked to contact the address given. Please bear in mind that most are run by volunteers — please enclose a stamped self-addressed envelope when writing and respect the privacy of individuals. This book does not grant or imply any permission whatsoever to enter premises to look at old buses except by the agreement of the group involved. Note that, where buses are licensed for use on public passenger-carrying services, the use of individual vehicles will vary from time to time, as the demands of their preservation dictate.

Whilst some of the restored vehicles detailed here have been 'officially' preserved by their former operators, the majority have been restored and conserved by volunteers, often working in difficult conditions with limited resources of time, money and materials. That there are so many buses and coaches fully restored is a testimony to the dedication of bus enthusiasts over the last 40 years or more, and it is intended that the vehicles will have a long and secure future.

The information used in this book is as provided by the organisations listed, for which the authors express their thanks. Any information on further collections not included in the current edition will be most welcome. If you own vehicles, or are associated wih such an organisation, please contact NARTM at the address given on page 5.

For each vehicle, details given include the present

Above: The Friends of King Alfred Buses organise an annual Running Day (usually 1 January), giving enthusiasts and members of the public the chance to ride on buses once operated by the late-lamented Winchester independent. 1970 Plaxton-bodied Leyland Panther UOU 419H was photographed in its home city on one such occasion. *Stephen Morris*

registration number, year first registered, brief chassis and body details (including seating) and original operator. Standard PSV Circle body codes are used, as outlined below.

Body type (before seating capacity):

A	articulated
B	single-deck bus
C	coach (single-deck)
CH	double-decker coach
Ch	charabanc
CO	convertible open-top double-decker
DP	dual-purpose (eg coach seats in bus shell)
F	full-front (where not normal for chassis)
H	Highbridge double-decker
L	Lowbridge double-decker (ie with sunken side gangway upstairs; all other types — with conventional gangways — are 'H', regardless of overall height)
O	open-top double-decker
OB	open-top single-decker
PO	partially-open-top double decker
R	single-decker with raised rear saloon (eg over luggage compartment)
T	Toastrack

Seating capacity:

For double-deckers this is shown with the upper-deck capacity first , eg 43/31

Door position (after seating capacity):

C	centre entrance/exit
D	dual doors (usually front entrance and centre exit)
F	front or forward entrance/exit
R	open rear platform
RD	rear entrance/exit with doors
RO	open rear platform with open staircase
T	triple doors (eg on articulated vehicles)

Suffix:

t	fitted with toilet
l	fitted with wheelchair lift

The restoration state is given in accordance with the following code:

R	restored;
RP	restoration in progress;
A	awaiting restoration.

Above: Also seen in Winchester on a FoKAB Running Day is AAA 756, a rare Albion Victor with centre-entrance Abbot coachwork, new to King Alfred in 1935. This vehicle is now kept at the Scottish Vintage Bus Museum at Lathalmond, Fife. *Stephen Morris*

An interesting line-up of vehicles, all of Bristol/ECW manufacture, from the Keighley Bus Museum. From left to right are former West Yorkshire FLF 1810 (KWT 642D), KSW recovery vehicle 4044 (LWR 424), RELH coach 2508 (TWW 766F) and RELL bus 1403 (OWT 776M), and former Southern National LS coach 1381 (SVS 904; originally OTT 90). *Stephen Morris*

Part 1
Museums Normally Open to the Public

Key to facilities

A	Audio/visual displays	H	Baby changing facilities
B	Bus rides (regular)	L	Lecture theatre
B(e)	Bus rides (at events)	M	Band stand
C	Children's information pack	P	Car parking
D	Access for disabled	R	Refreshments
E	Picnic facilities	S	Enthusiasts' shop
F	School activity pack	T	Toilets
G	Gift shop		

Abbey Pumping Station   Leicester

Contact address: Corporation Road, Leicester LE4 5PX
Phone: 0116 299 5111
Fax: 0116 299 5125

Brief description: The Museum is a Victorian pumping-station dating from 1892 with four beam-engines. The vehicle collection is on view on special open days. On these occasions, one of the beam-engines is steamed.

Events planned: Please see the enthusiast press for details.

Opening days/times:
Mon-Sat: 10.00 to 16.00 (17.00 in summer)
Sun: 14.00 to 16.30 (17.00 in summer)

Directions by car: A6 (north of Leicester) joins Abbey Lane at Redhill Island. Corporation Road is off Abbey Lane.

Directions by public transport: From City Centre (Charles Street) take bus 54 to top of Corporation Road.

Charges: Free except on special open days.

Facilities: C D E G H P R (on open days) T

Registration	Date	Chassis	Body	New to	Fleet No	Status
CBC 921	1939	AEC Renown O664	Northern Counties H32/32R	Leicester City Transport	329	R
GAY 171	1950	Leyland Tiger PS1/1	Willowbrook C35F	Allen, Mountsorrel	43	A
TBC 164	1958	Leyland Titan PD3/1	Willowbrook H41/33R	Leicester City Transport	164	R
MTL 750	1958	Leyland Tiger Cub PSUC1/2	Yeates DP43F	Delaine Coaches, Bourne	47	R
JMC 121K	1972	AEC Reliance 6MU4R	Plaxton C34C	Glenton Tours, London		R
OUM 727P	1976	Bedford J2SZ10	Caetano C16F	Anderton Tours, Keighley		R
B401 NJF	1984	Ford Transit 190D	Rootes B16F	Midland Fox	M1	R

Notes:
CBC 921   On view at Snibston Discovery Park

Above: 1958 Yeates-bodied Leyland Tiger Cub MTL 750 was formerly No 47 with 'The Delaine', the renowned Lincolnshire independent. *Philip Lamb*

Right: Former Southdown 517 (UF 1517), a 1927 Short-bodied Dennis 30cwt, is seen in Havant bus station on a Southdown Running Day. *Philip Lamb*

Amberley Museum

Contact address: Amberley, Arundel, West Sussex, BN18 9LT
Phone: 01798 831370
Fax: 01798 831831
E-mail: office@amberleymuseum.co.uk
Brief Description: The industrial museum has a wide range of attractions, including rail and bus operations. Some buses in the collection are museum-owned and others are owned by the Southdown Omnibus Trust or are in private hands.
Events planned: 19 September 2000 — Leyland 2000 Bus Show.
Opening days/times: March to October: Weds to Sun (also Mon and Tues during school holidays)
Directions by car: Situated close to Amberley railway station on the B2139. Approach from the north and west via the A29 and from the east via the A24 and A283.
Directions by public transport: Hourly rail service calls at Amberley station which is adjacent to the museum.
Charges: Adults £6.25, Over 60s/Students £5.50, Child £3.25, Family (2a+3c) £17.
Facilities: A B B(e) C D E F G H L P R T

Registration	Date	Chassis	Body		New to	Fleet No	Status
IB 552	1914	Tilling-Stevens TS3 Petrol-Electric	Newman O22/18R		Worthing Motor Services		R
CD 5125	1920	Leyland N	Short O27/24R		Southdown Motor Services	125	R
CD 4867	1923	Tilling-Stevens TS3A Petrol-Electric	(chassis only)				RP
BP 9822	1924	Shelvoke & Drewry Freighter	Hickman (replica) B18C		Tramocar, Worthing		R
UF 1517	1927	Dennis 30cwt	Short B19R		Southdown Motor Services	517	R
MO 9324	1927	Tilling-Stevens B9	Brush B32R		Thames Valley Traction Co	152	R
BR 7132	1929	Leyland Lion LT1	Leyland B34F		Sunderland Corporation	2	R
UF 6473	1930	Leyland Titan TD1	Leyland H24/24R		Southdown Motor Services	873	R
UF 6805	1930	Tilling-Stevens B10A2	Short B31R		Southdown Motor Services	1205	RP
UF 7428	1931	Leyland Titan TD1	Short H26/24R		Southdown Motor Services	928	R
EUF 184	1938	Leyland Titan TD5	Leyland		Southdown Motor Services	0184	

Notes:

IB 552	Petrol-electric transmission		
CD 5125	Rebodied 1928		
CD 4867	Petrol-electric. To be restored as Southdown replica		
BP 9822	Solid tyres. Replica body built at Amberley		
UF 1517	All-metal body		
MO 9324	Mechanical transmission. Replica body built at Amberley		

Aston Manor Road Transport Museum

Contact address: The Old Tram Depot, 208-216 Witton Lane, Aston, Birmingham B6 6QE
Phone: 0121 322 2298
Fax: 0121 368 0544
Affiliation: NARTM
Brief description: The 19th-century former tram depot houses a selection of buses, coaches, commercial vehicles and tramcar bodies in an authentic setting — the depot still has tram tracks and stone sets in situ. There are also many small exhibits, working model layouts and video presentations.
Events planned:
29 May 2000 — Two Museums Running Day. Bus service linking Aston Manor and Wythall.
9 July 2000 — Open day/vehicle gathering.
17 Sept 2000 — Outer Circle Rally at Cannon Hill Park.
26 Nov 2000 — Collectors' fair with free bus rides.
Please see the enthusiast press for other events.

Opening days/times:
Saturdays, Sundays and Bank Hols 11.00 to 17.00. Other times by arrangement.
Opening times may vary during September and over Christmas/New Year period.
Directions by car: Easy access from M6 junction 6.
Directions by public transport: Rail to Witton Station and a short walk (170yd)
Bus No 7 from Birmingham City Centre or bus No 11, outer circle to Witton Square.
Charges:
Adults £1, Child 50p, Family £2.75.
Admission charges may vary on special event days.
Facilities: A B(e) D P R S T
Other information: Not all of the vehicles listed are on display at the museum. To view any vehicle not normally accessible, visitors should enquire at the museum as to arrangements for viewing.

Registration	Date	Chassis	Body	New to	Fleet No	Status
*	1925	AEC S	Buckingham	Birmingham Corporation Tramways	215	A
OP 237	1926	(body only)	Short	Birmingham Corporation Tramways	208	A
EA 4181	1929	Dennis E	Dixon B32F	West Bromwich Corporation	32	RP
HA 4963	1930	SOS RR	Brush	BMMO ('Midland Red')	963	A
*	1930	SOS M	(chassis only)	BMMO ('Midland Red')		A
JF 2378	1931	AEC Regal 662	Burlingham C32R	Provincial, Leicester	R1	R
*	1931	SOS IM4	(chassis only)	BMMO ('Midland Red')		RP
OJ 9347	1933	Morris-Commercial Dictator	Metro-Cammell B—F	Birmingham Corporation Tramways	47	A
ANB 851	1934	Crossley Mancunian	Crossley/MCT H28/26R	Manchester Corporation	436	RP
AUF 670	1934	Leyland Titan TD3	East Lancs H26/26R	Southdown Motor Services	970	R
AOG 642	1935	Daimler COG5		Birmingham Corporation Tramways	3	A
AOG 679	1935	Daimler COG5		Birmingham Corporation Tramways	83	RP
CDH 501	1935	Dennis Lance	Park Royal H28/24R	Walsall Corporation	110	A
EHA 775	1938	SOS SON	English Electric	BMMO ('Midland Red')	2207	A
FON 630	1942	Leyland Titan TD7	(chassis only)	Birmingham City Transport	1330	A
HHA 26	1945	Guy Arab II	Weymann H30/26R	BMMO ('Midland Red')	2574	RP
DDM 652	1946	Maudslay Marathon II	Duple C33F	Rhyl United Coachways		R
GOE 486	1947	Daimler CVA6	Metro-Cammell H30/24R	Birmingham City Transport	1486	R
KHA 311	1948	BMMO C1	Duple C30C	BMMO ('Midland Red')	3311	R
KTT 689	1948	Guy Vixen	Wadham FC29F	Court Cars, Torquay		R
LKN 550	1949	Bedford OB	Mulliner B28F	Dineley, Margate		A
JHA 890	1949	BMMO S8	Metro-Cammell B40F	BMMO ('Midland Red')	3290	A
KHA 352	1950	BMMO CL2	Plaxton C26C	BMMO ('Midland Red')	3352	RP
LFM 724	1950	Bristol L5G	ECW B35R	Crosville Motor Services	KG143	A
SB 8155	1950	Guy Wolf	Ormac B20F	Alexander MacConnacher, Ballachulish		R
JOJ 222	1950	Leyland Titan PD2/1	Park Royal H29/25R	Birmingham City Transport	2222	RP
JOJ 231	1950	Leyland Tiger PS2	Weymann B34F	Birmingham City Transport	2231	R
JOJ 257	1950	Leyland Tiger PS2	Weymann B34F	Birmingham City Transport	2257	A
JOJ 526	1950	Guy Arab IV	Metro-Cammell H30/24R	Birmingham City Transport	2526	A
JOJ 548	1950	Guy Arab IV	Metro-Cammell H30/24R	Birmingham City Transport	2548	RP
KEL 131	1950	Leyland Titan PD2/3	Weymann FH33/25D	Bournemouth Corporation	131	RP
GUJ 608	1950	Sentinel STC4	Sentinel B40F	Sentinel demonstrator		R
MLL 584	1951	AEC Regal IV 9821LT	Metro-Cammell B37F	London Transport	RF197	R
JOJ 707	1951	Daimler CVD6	Metro-Cammell H30/24R	Birmingham City Transport	2707	R
RSK 615	1951	Leyland Royal Tiger PSU1/15	Duple DP41F	Jackson, Castle Bromwich		R
LLU 613	1952	AEC Regent III O961	Weymann H30/26R	London Transport	RT3254	RP
JOJ 847	1952	Daimler CVG6	Crossley H30/25RD	Birmingham City Transport	2847	A

Registration	Date	Chassis	Body	New to	Fleet No	Status
LOG 301	1952	Guy Arab IV	Saunders-Roe H30/25R	Birmingham City Transport	3001	RP
MOF 9	1953	Guy Arab IV	Metro-Cammell H30/25R	Birmingham City Transport	3009	R
LOG 302	1954	Daimler CLG5	Metro-Cammell H30/25R	Birmingham City Transport	3002	R
MOF 90	1954	Guy Arab IV	Metro-Cammell H30/25R	Birmingham City Transport	3090	RP
RRU 903	1955	Leyland Tiger Cub PSUC1/1	Park Royal B40F	Bournemouth Corporation	266	RP
773 FHA	1958	BMMO D9	BMMO H40/32RD	BMMO ('Midland Red')	4773	A
XVC 290	1959	Daimler CVG6	Metro-Cammell	Coventry Corporation	290	RP
1294 RE	1959	Guy Arab LUF	Burlingham C41F	Harper Bros, Heath Hayes	60	A
WLT 506	1960	AEC Routemaster R2RH	Park Royal H36/28R	London Transport	RM506	RP
RCK 920	1962	Leyland Titan PD3/5	Metro-Cammell FH41/31F	Ribble Motor Services	1775	R
6775 DD	1962	Leyland Leopard PSU3/1R	Plaxton C47F	Black & White Motorways	L225	
966 RVO	1963	Bedford VAL14	Yeates C50D	Barton Transport, Chilwell	966	R
3035 HA	1963	BMMO D9	BMMO O40/32RD	BMMO ('Midland Red')	5035	RP
6314 HA	1963	BMMO D9	BMMO H40/32RD	BMMO ('Midland Red')	5314	A
334 CRW	1963	Daimler CVG6	Metro-Cammell H34/29R	Coventry Corporation	334	RP
264 ERY	1963	Leyland Titan PD3A/1	Park Royal O41/33R	Leicester City Transport	264	R
6370 HA	1964	BMMO D9	BMMO H40/32RD	BMMO ('Midland Red')	5370	R
436 KOV	1964	Daimler Fleetline CRG6LX	Park Royal H43/33F	Birmingham City Transport	3436	A
EHA 415D	1966	BMMO D9	BMMO/Willowbrook H40/32RD	BMMO ('Midland Red')	5415	R
KOX 663F	1967	AEC Swift MP2R	MCW B37D	Birmingham City Transport	3663	RP
LHA 870F	1967	BMMO S21	BMMO DP49F	BMMO ('Midland Red')	5870	R
UHA 969H	1970	BMMO S23	BMMO/Plaxton B51F	BMMO ('Midland Red')	5969	A
XON 41J	1971	Daimler Fleetline CRG6LX	Park Royal H43/33F	West Midlands PTE	4041	R
HFL 672L	1973	Leyland Atlantean AN68/2R	Northern Counties H47/34F	Whippet Coaches, Fenstanton		R
JOV 714P	1975	Bristol VRTSL6LX	MCW H43/33F	West Midlands PTE	4714	R
WDA 700T	1979	Leyland Fleetline FE30AGR	MCW H43/33F	West Midlands PTE	7000	R
F685 YOG	1988	MCW Metrorider MF150/113	MCW B23F	West Midlands PTE	685	RP

Notes:

*	Registration not known
OJ 9347	Renumbered 77 in 1935
AUF 670	Rebodied in 1946
AOG 642	Originally bus 642 with BRCW H26/22R body; rebuilt as a lorry
AOG 679	Originally bus 679 with Northern Counties H26/22R body; rebodied 1947 as a van
ANB 851	Rebodied 1938
HHA 26	To be restored to wartime condition
KHA 352	Rebodied 1963
KEL 131	Built with twin staircases and dual doors
RSK 615	Originally registered LOE 300
LOG 302	Chrome-plated chassis exhibited 1952 Commercial Motor Show
RRU 903	Converted for OMO and rear door removed in 1957
XVC 290	Originally H33/27R; converted to towing vehicle
3035 HA	Originally H40/32RD; converted to open-top by Marshall ('Obsolete Fleet'), London (OM6)
264 ERY	Originally H41/33R

Right: An unusual vehicle at Aston Manor is SB 8155, a 1950 Ormac-bodied Guy Wolf.
Philip Lamb

Above: A survivor from Birmingham's prewar fleet of Daimler COG5s is Metro-Cammell-bodied 1107 (CVP 207), now resident at Wythall. *Philip Lamb*

Below: HWO 334 is a 1949 Guy Arab/Duple, delivered to Red & White Services when that company was still independent. Here it is keeping company with another 'independent' double-decker; Leyland PD3/MCW HBF 679D was new in 1966 to Harper Bros of Heath Hayes, which sold out to Midland Red in 1974. *Stephen Morris*

Birmingham & Midland Museum of Transport — Wythall

Contact address: Chapel Lane, Wythall, Worcestershire, B47 6JX
Phone: 01564 826471
E-mail: website: www.solnet.co.uk/bammot
Brief description: The collection is based on buses built and/or operated locally, plus others of significant PSV history. In addition, there is a unique collection of battery-operated road vehicles and a miniature passenger-carrying steam railway on site.
Events planned: Please see the enthusiast press for details.
Opening days/times: Saturdays, Sundays and Bank Holidays 11.00 to 17.00, Easter Sunday to 29 October, plus special open and operating days.

Directions by car: Wythall is on the main A435 Birmingham-Evesham road. The museum is next to Wythall Church. From M42 use junction 3 and head towards Birmingham.
Directions by public transport: Museum services operate on event days.
Midland Red West serves Wythall Island (not Sundays).
Wythall rail station is 25min walk from museum.
Charges: £1.50 but higher charges apply on open days.
Facilities: B(e) E P S T
Other information: Refreshments available on open days

Registration	Date	Chassis	Body	New to	Fleet No	Status
O 9926	1913	Tilling-Stevens TTA2	Tilling O18/16RO	BMMO ('Midland Red')	26	A
HA 3501	1925	SOS Standard	Ransomes, Simms & Jefferies B32F	BMMO ('Midland Red')	501	A
CN 2870	1927	SOS Q	Brush B37F	Northern General Transport Co	321	RP
CC 7745	1928	SOS QL	Brush B37F	Royal Blue, Llandudno		A
OV 4486	1931	AEC Regent I 661	Metro-Cammell H27/21R	Birmingham Corporation Tramways	486	A
OV 4090	1931	Morris-Commercial Dictator	Metro-Cammell B34F	Birmingham Corporation Tramways	90	A
OC 527	1933	Morris-Commercial Imperial	Metro-Cammell H—/—R	Birmingham Corporation Tramways	527	A
AHA 582	1935	SOS DON	Brush B36F	BMMO ('Midland Red')	1703	A
RC 4615	1937	AEC Regal O662	Willowbrook B35F	Trent Motor Traction Co	714	R
CVP 207	1937	Daimler COG5	Metro-Cammell H30/24R	Birmingham City Transport	1107	R
GHA 337	1940	SOS SON	Brush B38F	BMMO ('Midland Red')	2418	RP
HHA 637	1946	BMMO S6	Metro-Cammell B40F	BMMO ('Midland Red')	3036	A

Registration	Date	Chassis	Body	New to	Fleet No	Status
FFY 402	1947	Leyland Titan PD2/3	Leyland O30/26R	Southport Corporation	85	RP
JXC 432	1948	AEC Regent III O961	Weymann H30/26R	London Transport	RT624	A
KAL 579	1948	Daimler CVD6	Massey H33/28RD	W. Gash & Sons, Newark	DD2	R
FDM 724	1948	Foden PVD6	Massey H30/26R	E. H. Phillips Motor Services, Holywell		A
JRR 404	1948	Leyland Titan PD1	Duple L29/26R	Barton Transport, Chilwell	473	RP
GUE 247	1948	Leyland Tiger PS1	Northern Coachbuilders B34F	Stratford-upon-Avon Blue Motors	41	A
HOV 685	1948	Leyland Titan PD2/1	Brush H30/24R	Birmingham City Transport	1685	R
HDG 448	1949	Albion Venturer CX19	Metro-Cammell H30/26R	Cheltenham District Traction Co	72	R
HWO 334	1949	Guy Arab III	Duple L29/26R	Red & White Services	34	R
FJW 616	1949	Sunbeam F4	Park Royal H28/26R	Wolverhampton Corporation	616	A
NHA 744	1950	BMMO S12	Brush B44F	BMMO ('Midland Red')	3744	A
KFM 775	1950	Bristol L5G	ECW B35R	Crosville Motor Services	KG126	R
ORB 277	1950	Daimler CVD6	Duple C35F	Tailby & George ('Blue Bus Services'), Willington		R
JOJ 245	1950	Leyland Tiger PS2/1	Weymann B34F	Birmingham City Transport	2245	RP
JOJ 533	1950	Guy Arab IV	Metro-Cammell H30/24R	Birmingham City Transport	2533	R
JUE 349	1950	Leyland Tiger PS2/3	Northern Counties H35/28F	Stratford-upon-Avon Blue Motors	33	RP
NHA 795	1951	BMMO D5B	Brush H30/26RD	BMMO ('Midland Red')	3795	A
MXX 23	1952	AEC Regal IV 9821LT	Metro-Cammell B41F	London Transport	RF381	R
JOJ 976	1953	Guy Arab IV	Metro-Cammell H30/25R	Birmingham City Transport	2976	R
RDH 505	1953	Leyland Titan PD2/12	Roe FH33/23RD	Walsall Corporation	815	A
SHA 431	1953	Leyland Titan PD2/20	Leyland H30/26RD	BMMO ('Midland Red')	4031	RP
PDH 808	1953	Leyland Royal Tiger PSU1/13	Park Royal DP40F	Walsall Corporation	808	R
UHA 255	1955	BMMO S14	BMMO B44F	BMMO ('Midland Red')	4255	A
FRC 956	1955	Leyland Titan PD2/12	Leyland H32/26RD	Trent Motor Traction Co	1256	R
XHA 482	1956	BMMO D7	Metro-Cammell H37/26RD	BMMO ('Midland Red')	4482	A
XHA 496	1956	BMMO D7	Metro-Cammell	BMMO ('Midland Red')	4496	A
SUK 3	1957	Guy Arab IV	Metro-Cammell H33/27R	Wolverhampton Corporation	3	A
UTU 596J	1957	Guy Otter NLLODP	Mulliner B26F	Douglas Corporation	9	A
HFO 742	1958	Albion Victor FT39	Reading B35F	Guernsey Railway Co	62	R
VVP 911	1958	Bedford SB3	Duple C41F	Sandwell Motor Co, Birmingham		R
WDF 569	1959	Leyland Tiger Cub PSUC1/2	Willowbrook DP41F	Soudley Valley Coaches, Cinderford		RP
871 KHA	1960	BMMO D9	BMMO H40/32RD	BMMO ('Midland Red')	4871	A
943 KHA	1960	BMMO D10	BMMO H43/35F	BMMO ('Midland Red')	4943	R
802 MHW	1961	Bristol Lodekka FSF6G	ECW H34/26F	Cheltenham District Traction Co	6037	R
5073 HA	1962	BMMO S15	BMMO DP40F	BMMO ('Midland Red')	5073	R
248 NEA	1963	Daimler CVG6/30	Metro-Cammell H41/33R	West Bromwich Corporation	248	R
3016 HA	1963	BMMO D9	BMMO O40/32RD	BMMO ('Midland Red')	5016	R
6545 HA	1964	BMMO S16	BMMO B52F	BMMO ('Midland Red')	5545	R
CUV 219C	1965	AEC Routemaster R2RH/1	Park Royal H36/29RD	London Transport	RCL2219	R
BHA 399C	1965	BMMO D9	BMMO H40/32RD	BMMO ('Midland Red')	5399	R
BHA 656C	1965	BMMO CM6T	BMMO C44Ft	BMMO ('Midland Red')	5656	R
BON 474C	1965	Daimler Fleetline CRG6LX	Marshall B37F	Birmingham City Transport	3474	R
EHA 767D	1966	BMMO S17	BMMO/Plaxton B52F	BMMO ('Midland Red')	5767	R
GHA 415D	1966	Daimler Fleetline CRG6LX	Alexander H44/33F	BMMO ('Midland Red')	6015	A
GRY 60D	1966	Leyland Titan PD3A/1	Park Royal H41/33R	Leicester City Transport	60	A
HBF 679D	1966	Leyland Titan PD2A/27	MCW H36/28RD	Harper Bros, Heath Hayes	27	RP
JHA 868E	1967	BMMO S21	BMMO DP49F	BMMO ('Midland Red')	5868	A
KHW 306E	1967	Bristol RELL6L	ECW B53F	Cheltenham District Traction Co	1000	R
NJW 719E	1967	Daimler Roadliner SRC6	Strachans B54D	Wolverhampton Corporation	719	R
KOX 780F	1968	Daimler Fleetline CRG6LX	Park Royal H43/33F	Birmingham City Transport	3780	R
NEA 101F	1968	Daimler Fleetline CRG6LX	MCW H42/31F	West Bromwich Corporation	101	A
XDH 56G	1968	Daimler Fleetline CRC6-36	Northern Counties H51/34D	Walsall Corporation	56	RP
XDH 516G	1969	Daimler Fleetline CRG6LX	Northern Counties H41/27D	Walsall Corporation	116	R
OTA 632G	1969	Bristol RELH6G	ECW C45F	Southern National Omnibus Co (Royal Blue)	1460	R
SHA 645G	1969	Leyland Leopard PSU4A/4R	Plaxton C36F	BMMO ('Midland Red')	6145	A
UHA 956H	1970	BMMO S23	BMMO/Plaxton B51F	BMMO ('Midland Red')	5956	R
UHA 963H	1970	BMMO S23	BMMO/Plaxton B51F	BMMO ('Midland Red')	5963	R

Registration	Date	Chassis	Body	New to	Fleet No	Status
UHA 981H	1970	BMMO S23	BMMO/Plaxton B51F	BMMO ('Midland Red')	5981	R
WNG 864H	1970	Bristol RELL6G	ECW DP50F	Eastern Counties Omnibus Co	RLE864	A
FRB 211H	1970	Bristol VRTSL6LX	ECW H39/31F	Midland General Omnibus Co	322	R
OWE 271K	1972	Bristol VRTSL6LX	East Lancs H43/30F	Sheffield Transport	271	RP
CBD 778K	1972	Bristol VRTSL6LX	ECW H39/31F	United Counties Omnibus Co	778	R
TCH 274L	1973	Bristol RELH6G	ECW DP49F	Midland General Omnibus Co	274	R
PHA 370M	1974	Ford R1014	Plaxton/Midland Red DP23F	Midland Red Omnibus Co	370	A
GNU 569N	1974	Leyland National 11351/1R	Leyland National B49F	Trent Motor Traction Co	422	A
JMY 120N	1974	Leyland National 11351/1R/EXC	Leyland National C—Ft	National Travel		A
TOE 527N	1974	Ailsa B55-10	Alexander H44/35F	West Midlands PTE	4527	R
JOV 613P	1975	Daimler Fleetline CRG6LX	Park Royal H43/33F	West Midlands PTE	4613	R
99-64-HB	1976	Den Oudsten LOK	Den Oudsten B35D	VAD, Ermele (Netherlands)	5656	A
KON 311P	1976	Leyland Fleetline FE30ALR	MCW H43/33F	West Midlands PTE	6311	R
NOE 544R	1976	Leyland National 11351A/1R	Leyland National B49F	Midland Red Omnibus Co	544	RP
OJD 903R	1977	Leyland National 10351A/1R	Leyland National B36D	London Transport	LS103	R
BOK 1V	1979	MCW Metrobus DR102/12	MCW H43/30F	West Midlands PTE	2001	A
KVF 247V	1980	Bristol VRTSL3/6LXB	ECW H43/31F	Eastern Counties Omnibus Co	VR247	R

Notes:

RC 4615	Rebodied 1950	HFO 742	Originally registered 8231
FFY 402	Originally H30/26R	3016 HA	Originally H40/32RD; converted to open-top by Marshall ('Obsolete Fleet'), London (OM5)
KAL 579	Rebodied 1958		
FJW 616	Trolleybus	CBD 778K	Modified to resemble VRTSL3 by United Counties
JUE 349	Rebodied 1963	PHA 370M	Shortened by Midland Red in 1979
XHA 496	Converted to breakdown vehicle	99-64-HB	Netherlands registration
UTU 596J	Originally registered WMN 485	KON 311P	Gardner engine fitted in 1981

Above: One of the very few surviving Daimler Roadliners is NJW 719E, a Strachans-bodied example new in 1967 to Wolverhampton Corporation. *Stephen Morris*

The more modern vehicles at Wythall include a number of Bristol/ECW manufacture.

Above: Seen here are FRB 211H, a VR new to Midland General, OTA 632G, a one-time Southern National RELH used on Royal Blue express services, and KHW 306E, a former Cheltenham & District RELL. *Stephen Morris*

Below: Representing the National Bus Company era are TCH 274L, a dual-purpose RELH new to Midland General, and CBD 778K, a former United Counties VR. The latter's Series 3 front will be noted. *Stephen Morris*

British Commercial Vehicle Museum   Leyland

Contact address: King Street, Leyland, Lancashire, PR5 1LE
Phone: 01772 451011
Fax: 01772 623404
Brief description: A unique line-up of historic commercial vehicles and buses spans a century of truck and bus building. More than 50 exhibits are on display in this national collection.
Events planned: Please see the enthusiast press for details.
Opening days/times:
April to end of September: Sundays, Tuesdays, Wednesdays and

Bank Holidays, 10.00 to 17.00
October: Sundays only, 10.00 to 17.00
Directions by car: Close to the M6 Junction 28.
Directions by public transport:
By train to Leyland station (on West Coast main line).
Buses from Preston and Chorley bus stations.
Charges: Adult £4, Child/OAP £2, Family £10.
Facilities: A B(e) D F G L P R S T

Registration	Date	Chassis	Body	New to	Fleet No	Status
UL 1771	1929	Bean 30cwt	Birch B14F	Turner, Wandsworth		R
IF-14-62	1948	AEC Regal III O963	CCFL B16D	Carris, Lisbon	104	R
KYY 653	1950	AEC Regent III O961	Weymann H30/26R	London Transport	RT1798	R
XTC 684	1955	Leyland LFDD	Metro-Cammell H37/24RD	Leyland demonstrator		R
OED 217	1956	Foden PVD6	East Lancs H30/28R	Warrington Corporation	112	R
301 LJ+	1962	Sunbeam MF2B	Weymann H37/28D	Bournemouth Corporation	301	R
+ Trolleybus						

Notes:
IF-14-62   Portuguese registration; rebodied 1972

Above: The oldest bus on display at the British Commercial Vehicle Museum is UL 1771, a 1929 Birch-bodied Bean 30cwt. *Philip Lamb*

Castle Point Transport Museum   Canvey Island

Contact address: 105 Point Road, Canvey Island, Essex SS8 7TP
Phone: 01268 684272
E-mail: Glynis@topolino.demon.co.uk
Affiliation: NARTM
Brief description: This historic former Canvey & District bus depot, built in 1935, houses approximately 35 commercial vehicles spanning the years 1944 to 1972. Exhibits include buses, coaches, lorries, fire engines and military vehicles. They can be seen in varying stages from the totally restored to those in need of complete restoration. Completely run by volunteers, membership of the society is available at £6 per annum.

Events planned: 8 October 2000 — Annual Transport Show
Opening days/times: Open on Sundays, April to October.
Directions by car: A130 to Canvey Island; follow brown tourism signs on reaching the island.
Directions by public transport: By rail to South Benfleet, then by bus to Leigh Beck, Canvey Island.
Charges: Free admission. Donations welcome. A charge is made on the Transport Show day in October.
Facilities: B(e) P T
Other information: Hot drinks available.

Registration	Date	Chassis	Body	New to	Fleet No	Status
JVW 430	1944	Bristol K5G	ECW L27/28R	Eastern National Omnibus Co	3885	R
FOP 429	1944	Daimler CWA6	Duple O33/26R	Birmingham Corporation Tramways	1429	R
MPU 52	1947	Leyland Titan PD1A	ECW L27/26R	Eastern National Omnibus Co	3991	RP
CFV 851	1948	Bedford OB	Duple C29F	Seagull Coaches, Blackpool		R
KGU 413	1949	AEC Regent III O961	Weymann H30/26R	London Transport	RT1544	R
LYR 997	1949	AEC Regent III O961	Weymann H30/26R	London Transport	RT2827	R
LHY 937	1949	Bristol K6B	ECW H31/28R	Bristol Tramways & Carriage Co	C3448	RP
NEH 453	1949	Leyland Titan OPD2/1	Northern Counties L27/26RD	Potteries Motor Traction Co	L453	R
ONO 49	1950	Bristol L5G	ECW B35R	Eastern National Omnibus Co	4029	R
PTW 110	1950	Bristol L6B	ECW FC31F	Eastern National Omnibus Co	4107	RP
VRF 372	1951	Foden PVRF6	Harrington C41C	Bassett's Coachways, Tittensor		RP
WNO 478	1953	Bristol KSW5G	ECW O33/28R	Westcliff-on-Sea Motor Services		R
OLD 717	1954	AEC Regent III O961	Weymann H30/26R	London Transport	RT4497	R
XVX 19	1954	Bristol Lodekka LD5G	ECW H33/25R	Eastern National Omnibus Co	4208	R
JAP 698	1954	Harrington Contender	Harrington C41C	Audawn Coaches, Corringham		RP
381 BKM	1957	AEC Reliance MU3RV	Harrington C41F	Maidstone & District Motor Services	C381	RP
PHJ 954	1958	Leyland Titan PD3/6	Massey L35/33R	Southend Corporation	315	RP
UHJ 842	1959	Bedford C4Z2	Duple C29F	Rochford Hospital (staff bus)		A
236 LNO	1959	Bristol Lodekka LDL6G	ECW H37/33R	Eastern National Omnibus Co	1541	A
217 MHK	1959	Bristol MW6G	ECW DP41F	Eastern National Omnibus Co	480	R
SGD 407	1960	Leyland Titan PD3/2	Alexander H41/31F	Glasgow Corporation	L405	RP
373 WPU	1961	Guy Arab IV	Massey L34/33R	Moore Bros, Kelvedon		R
28 TKR	1962	AEC Reliance 2MU3RV	Harrington C29F	Maidstone & District Motor Services	C28	R
138 CLT	1962	AEC Routemaster R2RH	Park Royal H36/28R	London Transport	RM1138	RP
918 NRT	1963	AEC Regent V MD3RV	Massey H32/28RD	Lowestoft Corporation	8	RP
SDX 57	1963	AEC Regent V 2D2RA	Neepsend H37/28R	Ipswich Corporation	57	RP
CUV 233C	1965	AEC Routemaster R2RH/1	Park Royal H36/29RD	London Transport	RCL2233	R
NTW 942C	1965	Bristol Lodekka FLF6G	ECW H38/32F	Eastern National Omnibus Co	2849	R
AVX 975G	1968	Bristol Lodekka FLF6LX	ECW H38/32F	Eastern National Omnibus Co	2614	RP
CPU 979G	1969	Bristol VRTSL6LX	ECW H39/31F	Eastern National Omnibus Co	3000	R

Notes:

JVW 430	Renumbered 1274 in 1954
FOP 429	Originally H33/26R; later operated by Eastern National Omnibus Co and Southend Corporation (244)
MPU 52	Renumbered 1121 in 1954
LHY 937	Renumbered 1541 in 1964
ONO 49	Renumbered 309 in 1954 and 1107 in 1964
PTW 110	Renumbered 328 in 1954
WNO 478	Built as H33/28R; numbered 1423 in 1954, passed to

	Eastern National Omnibus Co in 1955, renumbered 2380 in 1964 and converted to open-top in 1965/6
XVX 19	Renumbered 1431 in 1954 and 2400 in 1964
JAP 698	Former Harrington demonstrator
236 LNO	Renumbered 2510 in 1964
217 MHK	Renumbered 1402 in 1964
AVX 975G	Delivered as CH37/18F; fitted with bus seats and renumbered 2946 in 1969

Above: The Castle Point Transport Museum is based at the former Canvey & District depot vacated by Eastern National in 1978. Standing in the entrance is NEH 453, a lowbridge Northern Counties-bodied Leyland Titan new to Potteries in 1949 and unusual in being based on an OPD2 (export) chassis. *Andy Izatt*

City of Portsmouth Preserved Transport Depot

Contact address: 48-54 Broad Street, Portsmouth PO1 2JE
Phone: 02392 818223
Fax: 02392 256602
E-mail: friends@cpptd.freeserve.co.uk
Affiliation: NARTM
Brief description: 21 veteran and vintage buses, trams and trolleybuses are on display, most of which spent their working lives in the south of England. Up to 10 are available for bus rides on open days.
Events planned: Open days on second and last Sunday of every month.

Opening days/times: Second and last Sunday of every month: 10.00 to 17.00
Directions by car: From M275 follow directions for Isle of Wight car ferry. At Cambridge Road roundabout go straight ahead. Museum is in Broad Street on right-hand side.
Directions by public transport: Bus 16A from Portsmouth Harbour station. Free vintage bus service on open days.
Charges: Free
Facilities: B B(e) C D F S T
Other information: Car parking nearby (fee payable)

Registration	Date	Chassis	Body	New to	Fleet No	Status
*	1876	Horse bus		G. Wheeler, Fawley		A
BK 2986	1919	Thornycroft J	Dodson O18/16R	Portsmouth Corporation	10	R
RV 3411	1933	Leyland Titan TD2	-	Portsmouth Corporation	17	R
RV 4649+	1934	AEC 661T	English Electric H26/24R	Portsmouth Corporation	201	RP
RV 6368	1935	Leyland Titan TD4	English Electric O26/24R	Portsmouth Corporation	8	R
ECD 524	1937	Leyland Cub KPZ2	Park Royal B20F	Southdown Motor Services	24	RP
EHO 228	1942	Guy Arab I	Reading H30/26R	Gosport & Fareham Omnibus Co	55	R
CTP 200	1944	Bedford OWB	Duple (replica) B32F	Portsmouth Corporation	170	R
DTP 823	1947	Leyland Titan PD1	Weymann H30/26R	Portsmouth Corporation	189	RP
AHC 442	1951	AEC Regent III 9613A	Bruce H30/26R	Eastbourne Corporation	42	R
EHV 65	1951	Bedford OB	Duple B29F	East Ham Borough Council		R
LRV 996	1956	Leyland Titan PD2/12	Metro-Cammell O33/26R	Portsmouth Corporation	4	R
ORV 989	1958	Leyland Titan PD2/40	Metro-Cammell H30/26R	Portsmouth Corporation	112	RP
PRX 206B	1964	Leyland Titan PD3/4	Northern Counties FCO39/30F	Southdown Motor Services	401	R
BBK 236B	1964	Leyland Atlantean PDR1/1	Metro-Cammell H43/33F	Portsmouth Corporation	236	R
TBK 190K	1971	Leyland Atlantean PDR2/1	Seddon B40D	Portsmouth Corporation	190	R
JWV 275W	1981	Bristol VRTSL3/680	ECW H43/31F	Southdown Motor Services	275	RP

+ Trolleybus

Notes:

*	Not registered
BK 2986	Body is c1910 ex-LGOC B-type
RV 3411	Converted to tower wagon in 1955
RV 6368	Originally H26/24R
EHO 228	Rebodied 1955
CTP 200	Replica body; wartime livery
EHV 65	Preserved in Hants & Sussex livery
LRV 996	Originally H33/26R
PRX206B	Originally registered 401 DCD

Right: Guy Arab chassis, with utility bodywork by various builders, were delivered to many operators during World War 2. EHO 228 was supplied to Gosport & Fareham ('Provincial') in 1942, and was rebodied by Reading in 1955. *Philip Lamb*

Above: Former Eastbourne 42 (AHC 442) is a 1951 AEC Regent III with handsome (and rare) Bruce bodywork.
Philip Lamb

Below: Former Portsmouth 236 (BBK 236B), a Leyland Atlantean/Metro-Cammell delivered in 1964.
Stephen Morris

Cobham Bus Museum

Contact address: Redhill Road, Cobham, Surrey, KT11 1EF
Phone/Fax: 01932 868665
Affiliation: NARTM
Brief description: This well-established museum was formed by a small group of enthusiasts in 1966. The collection has steadily grown over the years and now over 30 preserved buses are located at Cobham.
Events planned: Please see the enthusiast press for details.
Opening days/times: Open days as advertised.

Viewing possible at weekends 11.00 to 17.00 but please telephone in advance to confirm.
Directions by car: From M25 junction 10 take A3 north and turn left on to A245. Museum is 1 mile on left.
Directions by public transport: Museum bus service from Weybridge station on main events.
Infrequent bus service at other times to Brooklands Road/Byfleet.
Charges: £2 but higher charges on open days.
Facilities: B B(e) G P R(limited) S T

Registration	Date	Chassis	Body	New to	Fleet No	Status
XX 9591	1925	Dennis 4-ton	Dodson O24/24RO	Dominion Omnibus Co		R
UU 6646	1929	AEC Regal O662	LGOC B30R	London General Omnibus Co	T31	R
GJ 2098	1930	AEC Regent I 661	Tilling H27/25RO	Thomas Tilling		R
AXM 693	1934	AEC Regent I 661	LPTB H30/26R	London Transport	STL441	R
LJ 9501	1934	Albion Valiant PV70	Harrington C32F	Charlie's Cars, Bournemouth	57	RP
CGJ 188	1935	AEC Q O762	BRCW B35C	London Transport	Q83	R
CXX 171	1936	AEC Regal O662	Weymann C30F	London Transport	T448	RP
DLU 92	1937	AEC Regent I O661	LPTB H30/26R	London Transport	STL2093	A
ELP 228	1938	AEC Regal O662	LPTB C30F	London Transport	T504	R
EGO 426	1938	AEC Regent I O661	LPTB H30/26R	London Transport	STL2377	RP
HGC 130	1945	Guy Arab II	Park Royal H30/26R	London Transport	G351	RP
HLX 410	1948	AEC Regent III O961	Weymann H30/26R	London Transport	RT593	R
HLX 462	1948	AEC Regal III 9612E	Mann Egerton B31F	London Transport	T792	A
UMP 227	1949	AEC Regal IV	Park Royal B40F	AEC prototype		A
MYA 590	1949	Leyland Comet CPO1	Harrington C29F	Scarlet Pimpernel, Minehead		R
JXC 288	1949	Leyland Tiger PS1	Mann Egerton B30F	London Transport	TD95	R
KGK 803	1949	Leyland Titan PD2/1 ('7RT')	Park Royal H30/26R	London Transport	RTL139	R
LUC 210	1951	AEC Regal IV 9821LT	Metro-Cammell DP35F	London Transport	RF10	RP
LYR 826	1952	AEC Regent III O961	Park Royal H30/26R	London Transport	RT2775	RP
LYR 910	1952	AEC Regent III O961	Park Royal H30/26R	London Transport	RT3491	R
MLL 685	1952	Leyland Titan PD2/1 ('7RT')	Park Royal H30/26R	London Transport	RTL1323	A
MLL 969	1952	AEC Regal IV 9821LT	Metro-Cammell	London Transport	RF332	R
NLE 534	1952	AEC Regal IV 9821LT	Metro-Cammell B39F	London Transport	RF534	R
NLE 672	1953	AEC Regal IV 9821LT	Metro-Cammell B41F	London Transport	RF672	R
MLL 740	1953	AEC Regal IV 9822E	Park Royal RDP37C	British European Airways	1095	R
MXX 334	1953	Guy Special NLLVP	ECW B26F	London Transport	GS34	R
CDX 516	1954	AEC Regent III 9613E	Park Royal H30/26R	Ipswich Corporation	16	R
SLT 58	1957	Leyland Routemaster	Weymann H36/28R	London Transport	RML3	R
EGN 369J	1971	AEC Swift 4MP2R	Park Royal B33+34D	London Transport	SMS369	R
JPA 190K	1972	AEC Reliance 6U2R	Park Royal DP45F	London Country Bus Services	RP90	R
SPK 203M	1973	AEC Reliance 6U3ZR	Plaxton C49F	London Country Bus Services	P3	R

Notes:

XX 9591	Restored as London General Omnibus Co D142
GJ 2098	On loan to BMMO during World War 2
CXX 171	Used as an ambulance during World War 2
DLU 92	Original metal-framed Park Royal body replaced in 1949
ELP 228	Used as an ambulance during World War 2
HGC 130	Only remaining example of a London utility bus
UMP 227	Prototype AEC Regal IV — operated with London Transport in 1950

MYA 590	Converted from petrol to diesel in 1966
JXC 288	Toured Europe and USSR 1963-7
LYR 826	Toured USA and Canada when new
MLL 969	Converted to a towing vehicle in 1976
SLT 58	Prototype Leyland Routemaster; renumbered RM3 in 1961

Above: London Transport's GS class of ECW-bodied Guy Specials originally numbered 84; one of a number of survivors is Cobham Bus Museum's GS34 (MXX 334) of 1953.
Philip Lamb

Right: Leyland supplied London Transport with the RTL class, based on the manufacturer's PD2 model but heavily modified to achieve similarity with the more numerous RT class AEC Regents; the resultant chassis are often referred to as '7RT's, this being LT's engineering designation. RTL1323 (MLL 685) is preserved at Cobham; like the GS above, it carries LT Country Area green livery. *Philip Lamb*

Dover Transport Museum Whitfield

Contact address: Old Park, Whitfield, Dover, CT16 2HQ
Phone: 01304 822409/204612
Affiliation: NARTM, Transport Trust, AIM, ASTRO
Brief description: The museum displays local transport and social history. Road vehicles of all types. A maritime room, railway room, bygone shops and a garage. Hundreds of transport models including a working model tramway.
Events planned: Please see the enthusiast press for details.
Opening days/times: Easter to end June — Sundays 10.30 to 17.00;

July, August and September — Thursdays and Fridays 14.00 to 17.00; Sundays 10.30 to 17.00.
Open at other times for pre-arranged groups.
Directions by car: Approximately one mile from the A2 Whitfield roundabout on the Dover bypass.
Directions by public transport: Dover Priory station then bus to Old Park, Whitfield.
Charges: Adult £2, Senior Citizen £1.50, Child £1, Family £5.
Facilities: B(e) D E G P R T

Registration	Date	Chassis	Body	New to	Fleet No	Status
CC 9305	1929	Dennis GL	Roberts T19	Llandudno UDC		R
WYJ 813	1934	Renault TN6C	STRC B33R	RATP, Paris	2765	R
JG 9938	1937	Leyland Tiger TS8	Park Royal C32R	East Kent Road Car Co		R
KHY 383	1948	Bristol L6B	BBW B35R	Bristol Tramways & Carriage Co	2382	R
KXW 488	1950	AEC Regent III O961	Weymann H30/26R	London Transport	RT1389	RP
KYY 872	1950	AEC Regent III O961	Weymann H30/26R	London Transport	RT3143	R
EFN 591	1950	Dennis Lancet J3	Park Royal C32F	East Kent Road Car Co		A
FNV 557	1950	Leyland Tiger PS2/3	Whitson FC33F	Church ('Royal Blue'), Pytchley		R
NKT 896	1951	Leyland Titan PD2/12	Leyland H30/28RD	Maidstone & District Motor Services	DH400	A
FFN 451	1951	Leyland Royal Tiger PSU1/13	Park Royal C37C	East Kent Road Car Co		RP
GFN 273	1952	Beadle-Leyland	Beadle C35F	East Kent Road Car Co		R
PHJ 953	1958	Leyland Titan PD3/6	Massey O41/33R	Southend Corporation	314	R
569 KKK	1960	AEC Reliance 2MU3RA	Duple C41C	Ayers Coaches, Dover		R
WFN 513	1961	AEC Reliance 2MU3RV	Park Royal DP41F	East Kent Road Car Co		R
NSK 871	1961	Daimler CVG6	Roe O37/28R	Swindon Corporation	120	R
6801 FN	1961	AEC Regent V 2D3RA	Park Royal H40/32F	East Kent Road Car Co		R
AFN 780B	1963	AEC Regent V 2D3RA	Park Royal H40/30F	East Kent Road Car Co		R
GJG 739D	1966	AEC Regent V 2D3RA	Park Royal H40/32F	East Kent Road Car Co		A
GJG 751D	1966	AEC Regent V 2D3RA	Park Royal PO40/32F	East Kent Road Car Co		R
JRJ 268E	1967	Leyland Titan PD2/40	MCW H36/28F	Salford City Transport	268	R
GFN 546N	1975	Leyland National 10351/1R	Leyland National B40F	East Kent Road Car Co	1546	RP

Notes:

JG 9938	Restored in livery of subsequent owner Smith's of Sittingbourne
KHY 383	Carries 1950 body
EFN 591	Operated as a single-deck bus from June 1961

GFN 273	Rebuild of Leyland Titan TD5
PHJ 953	Originally L35/33R; converted to open-top in 1971
NSK 871	Originally registered XMW 120
GJG 751D	Originally H40/32F; used as promotional vehicle

Left: Park Royal-bodied Leyland Tiger JG 9938 was new to East Kent in 1938, but later passed to independent operator Smith's of Sittingbourne, in whose livery it is now preserved. *Stephen Morris*

Above right: Beadle-Leyland GFN 273 was nominally new to East Kent in 1952, but is in fact based on prewar Leyland TD5 mechanical components. *Philip Lamb*

Right: Former East Kent AEC Reliance/Park Royal WFN 513 was new in 1961. Like GFN 273, it is seen in Canterbury bus station, and makes for an interesting comparison in styling. *Philip Lamb*

Contact address: Chapel Road, Carlton Colville, Lowestoft, Suffolk, NR33 8BL
Phone: 01502 518459
Affiliation: NARTM & London Trolleybus Preservation Society.
Brief description: A working transport museum on a four-acre site, first opened in 1972 and run entirely by volunteers. Tram and trolley-bus services operate regularly within a developing street scene and the tramway has a woodland section. There is also a narrow-gauge railway. A wide variety of other vehicles on display and sometimes operated includes buses, lorries, steam rollers, battery-electrics, tower wagons and a London taxi. The museum is a registered charity.
Events planned: Please see the enthusiast press for details.
Opening days/times: At Easter, then from May to September: Sundays and Bank Holidays — 11.00 to 17.30;

Wednesdays and Saturdays (June to Sept) — 14.00 to 17.00; All other days (late July and Aug) — 14.00 to 17.00.
Directions by car: Situated on the A1384. Follow the brown signs from the A12, A146 and A1117.
Directions by public transport:
Monday to Saturday: Eastern Counties bus L11 or L12 from Lowestoft bus station to Carlton Colville Church, then 8min walk.
Sundays and Bank Holidays: Eastern Counties bus L18 or L19 from Lowestoft bus station to the Museum.
By train to Oulton Broad South then 35min walk.
Charges: £4.50 adults, £3 children/OAPs. Higher charges at special events. Admission includes free rides within the museum.
Facilities: B(e) D E F G H P R S T
Other information: Regular tram and trolleybus rides

Registration	Date	Chassis	Body	New to	Fleet No	Status
AH 79505+	1926	Garrett O type	Strachan & Brown B26D	NESA (Copenhagen)	5	RP
KW 1961	1927	Leyland Lion PLSC3	Leyland B35F	Blythe & Berwick, Bradford		A
CUL 260+	1936	AEC 664T	Metro-Cammell H40/30R	London Transport	260	R
EXV 201+	1938	Leyland LPTB70	Leyland H40/30R	London Transport	1201	R
FXH 521+	1940	Metro-Cammell	Metro-Cammell H40/30R	London Transport	1521	R
GBJ 192	1947	AEC Regent II O661	ECW H30/26R	Lowestoft Corporation	21	R
*	1948	Berna	Hess B37D	Biel (Switzerland)	39	R
KAH 408	1948	Bristol L4G	ECW B35R	Eastern Counties Omnibus Co	LL108	A
BDY 809+	1948	Sunbeam W	Weymann H30/26R	Hastings Tramways Co	34	RP
NBB 628+	1950	BUT 9641T	Metro-Cammell H40/30R	Newcastle Corporation	628	A
LLU 829	1950	Leyland Titan PD2/1 ('7RT')	Park Royal H30/26R	London Transport	RTL1050	A
ERV 938+	1951	BUT 9611T	Burlingham H28/26R	Portsmouth Corporation	313	A
SG 2030+	1952	Henschel Uh111/S	Uerdingen B32T	Solingen (Germany)	1	R
LCD 52+	1953	BUT 9611T	Weymann H30/26R	Brighton Corporation	52	R
DRC 224+	1953	Sunbeam F4	Willowbrook H32/28R	Derby Corporation	224	R
YTE 826+	1956	BUT 9612T	Bond H32/28R	Ashton-under-Lyne Corporation	87	R
2206 OI+	1958	Sunbeam F4A	Harkness H36/32R	Belfast Corporation	246	RP
YLJ 286+	1959	Sunbeam MF2B	Weymann H35/28D	Bournemouth Corporation	286	R
VRD 186+	1961	Sunbeam F4A	Burlingham H38/30F	Reading Corporation	186	R
557 BNG	1962	Bristol Lodekka FL6G	ECW H37/33RD	Eastern Counties Omnibus Co	LFL57	R
YRT 898H	1969	AEC Swift 2MP2R	ECW B45D	Lowestoft Corporation	4	R
OCK 985K	1972	Bristol VRTSL6LX	ECW H39/31F	Ribble Motor Services	1985	R

+ Denotes trolleybus

Notes:

AH 79505	Danish registration; being renovated in Copenhagen	2206 OI	Fitted with hydraulic brakes
*	Unregistered	OCK 985K	Acquired by Eastern Counties Omnibus Co (VR385)
SG 2030	German registration		in 1985
LCD 52	Built 1950, first used 1953; preserved in colours of subsequent operator Maidstone Corporation		

Right: The East Anglia Transport Museum at Carlton Colville is represented by former London Transport all-Leyland trolleybus 1201 (EXV 201) of 1938 and former Lowestoft AEC Regent/ECW 21 (GBJ 192) of 1947. The combination of AEC chassis and ECW bodywork is noteworthy; shortly after the bus was delivered, ECW bodies were restricted to nationalised fleets, and Lowestoft could no longer patronise its local bodybuilder. *John Robinson*

Imperial War Museum   London

Contact address: Lambeth Road, London SE1 6HZ
Phone:
0207 416 5320
0891 600140 (Recorded information)
E-mail: website: www.iwm.org.uk
Brief description: Revel in the history of the nation, through the world wars and much more besides. Regular exhibitions and displays of considerable educational value. The one bus in the collection fills a significant gap in transport history. Enquire before visiting on 020 7416 5211 to check bus is on display.
Opening days/times: Daily 10.00 to 18.00 (closed 24, 25 and 26 December)

Directions by car: South of Waterloo Station, close to the Elephant & Castle. Parking difficult but Coach Park at Vauxhall Bridge and disabled parking by prior arrangement only — phone 0207 416 5397.
Directions by public transport:
Underground to Lambeth North, Waterloo or Elephant & Castle.
Rail to Waterloo.
Bus routes 1, 3, 12, 45, 53, 63, 68, 159, 168, 171, 172, 176, 188, 344 and C10.
Charges: Adult £5.20, Senior Citizen £4.20, Children free. Group rates available. Free after 16.30 daily.
Facilities: A C D G H R T

Registration	Date	Chassis	Body	New to	Fleet No	Status
LN 4743	1911	LGOC B	LGOC O18/16RO	London General Omnibus Co	B43	R

Named *Ole Bill* after wartime cartoon character

38

Ipswich Transport Museum

Contact address: Old Trolleybus Depot, Cobham Road, Ipswich
IP3 9JD
Phone: 01473 715666
Fax: 01473 832260
E-mail: www.geocities.com/MotorCity/Downs/8806.html
Website: www.ipswichtransportmuseum.co.uk
Affiliation: NARTM, ASTRO, TORA, SEMS, AFSM
Brief description: The collection includes most forms of road transport from the last 200 years, including bicycles, horse-drawn vehicles, trucks and service vehicles. There are displays of vehicles and other products of Ipswich engineering companies including six mobile cranes.
Events planned: 14 May 2000 — Fiftieth anniversary of first Ipswich motor bus

15 October 2000 — Annual 'ride on our buses' day
Opening days/times: April to November: Sundays and Bank Holidays 11.00 to 16.30
August and school half-term, Monday to Friday 13.00 to 16.00
Directions by car: From A12/A14 junction with A1189 (Nacton and Ipswich East) head towards Ipswich on Nacton Road. Turn right into Lindburgh Road. Museum is on left in Cobham Road.
Directions by public transport: By train to Ipswich. Take any bus to Town Centre.
Then take bus 2 to Cobham Road (Mon-Fri) or bus 75/76/77 (Suns) to Felixstowe Road Railway bridge.
Charges: Adult £2.25, Child £1.25, Concessions £1.75, Family £6.
Facilities: A B(e) D G P R T

Registration	Date	Chassis	Body	New to	Fleet No	Status
DX 3988+	1923	Railless	Short B30D	Ipswich Corporation	2	R
DX 5629+	1926	Garrett O type	Strachan & Brown B31D	Ipswich Corporation	26	A
DX 5610+	1926	Ransomes, Simms & Jefferies D	Ransomes, Simms & Jefferies B31D	Ipswich Corporation	9	A
* +	1926	Ransomes, Simms & Jefferies	(chassis only)	Ipswich Corporation	16	R
DX 6591	1927	Tilling-Stevens B9B	Eastern Counties B36R	Eastern Counties Road Car Co	78	A
VF 2788	1928	ADC 425A	Eastern Counties B36R	United Automobile Services	J379	A
DX 7812	1929	Tilling-Stevens B10A2	(chassis only)	Eastern Counties Road Car Co	116	R
WV 1209	1932	Bedford WLB	Waveney B20F	Alexander, Devizes		A
PV 817+	1933	Ransomes, Simms & Jefferies	Ransomes, Simms & Jefferies H24/24R	Ipswich Corporation	46	A
CVF 874	1939	Bristol L5G	ECW B35R	Eastern Counties Omnibus Co	LL574	A
CAH 923	1940	Dennis Ace	ECW B20F	Eastern Counties Omnibus Co	D23	RP
PV 8270+	1948	Karrier W	Park Royal H30/26R	Ipswich Corporation	105	A
PV 9371	1949	Bedford OB	Duple C27F	Mulleys Motorways, Ixworth		R
KAH 407	1949	Bristol L4G	ECW B35R	Eastern Counties Omnibus Co	LL407	RP
ADX 1	1950	AEC Regent III 9612E	Park Royal H30/26R	Ipswich Corporation	1	R
ADX 196+	1950	Sunbeam F4	Park Royal H30/26R	Ipswich Corporation	126	R
MAH 744	1951	Bristol LSX4G	ECW B42F	Eastern Counties Omnibus Co	LL744	R
BPV 9	1953	AEC Regal IV 9822E	Park Royal B42D	Ipswich Corporation	9	A
BPV 10	1953	AEC Regal IV 9822E	(chassis only)	Ipswich Corporation	10	A
ADX 63B	1964	AEC Regent V 2D2RA	Massey H37/28R	Ipswich Corporation	63	R
APW 829B	1964	Bristol MW6G	ECW C39F	Eastern Counties Omnibus Co	LS829	R
CNG 125C	1965	Bristol Lodekka FS5G	ECW H33/27RD	Eastern Counties Omnibus Co	LFS125	RP
DPV 68D	1966	AEC Regent V 2D2RA	Neepsend H37/28R	Ipswich Corporation	68	A
JRT 82K	1971	AEC Swift 2MP2R	Willowbrook B40D	Ipswich Corporation	82	R
MRT 6P	1976	Leyland Atlantean AN68/1R	Roe H43/29D	Ipswich Corporation	6	R

+ Trolleybus

Notes:

DX 3988	Believed the oldest on display in the world	PV 817	First Ipswich double-decker
DX 5610	Changed from solid to pneumatic tyres in 1930	CVF 874	Originally numbered LL74
*	Unregistered	CAH 923	Originally fitted with Gardner 4LK engine
DX 6591	New with charabanc body; rebuilt in 1934	PV 8270	Originally fitted with wooden seats
VF 2788	Original United body replaced in 1934	ADX 1	Ipswich Corporation's first motor bus
DX 7812	Rebodied twice while with Eastern Counties	MAH 744	Bristol LS prototype

Left: The Ipswich Transport Museum includes one-time Eastern Counties LL744 (MAH 744). Delivered in 1951, it is one of two Bristol LS/ECW prototypes, recognisable by the unusual shape of windscreen. Happily, its fellow also survives, at the Dewsbury Bus Museum. *Philip Lamb*

Above: Seen undergoing a repaint in Tilling green livery is YDL 318, a 1962 Bristol FS/ECW. New as Southern Vectis 573, it is still owned by the company, and loaned to the Isle of Wight Bus Museum. *Stephen Morris*

Right: Southern Vectis 806 (FDL 927D) is an ECW-bodied Bristol MW, delivered in 1966. It is seen here in Newport on the occasion of the 1998 Running Day. *Philip Lamb*

Isle of Wight Bus Museum   Newport (IoW)

Contact address: Seaclose Quay, Newport, Isle of Wight, PO30 2EF
Phone: 01983 533352
Affiliation: NARTM
Brief description: The collection ranges from a 1927 Daimler CK to a 1985 Ford Transit. Many of the vehicles are of Southern Vectis origin.
Events planned: Please see the enthusiast press for details.
Opening days/times: End May to end September: Sunday to Friday, 10.30 to 16.00
Directions by car: Access off Medina Way relief road and Sea Street.

Left on to Quay. Bus museum is adjacent to Boat Museum (both signposted).
Directions by public transport: Bus to Newport bus station. Walk 12min to north of town.
Charges: £2 Adult, £1.50 Senior Citizen, £1 child.
Facilities: B(e) D G S
Other information: Car parking nearby. Refreshments and toilets at adjacent Boat Museum.

Registration	Date	Chassis	Body	New to	Fleet No	Status
DL 5084	1927	Daimler CK	Dodson B26R	Dodson Bros ('Vectis')	11	A
NG 1109	1931	Reo Pullman	Taylor C26D	Reynolds, Overstrand		R
DL 9015	1934	Dennis Ace	Harrington B20F	Southern Vectis Omnibus Co	405	RP
AUF 666	1934	Leyland Titan TD3	Beadle H28/26R	Southdown Motor Services	966	RP
JT 8077	1937	Bedford WTB	Duple C25F	South Dorset Coaches		R
EDL 657	1947	Bristol K5G	ECW L27/28R	Southern Vectis Omnibus Co	721	RP
HDL 279	1951	Bristol LL5G	ECW B39R	Southern Vectis Omnibus Co	835	RP
MDL 954	1956	Bristol Lodekka LD6G	ECW O33/27R	Southern Vectis Omnibus Co	544	R
ODL 399	1957	Bedford SBG	Duple C41F	Moss Motor Tours, Sandown		RP
PDL 515	1958	Bristol MW6G	ECW C39F	Southern Vectis Omnibus Co	315	RP
PDL 519	1958	Bristol Lodekka LD6G	ECW CO33/27R	Southern Vectis Omnibus Co	559	A
SDL 268	1959	Bristol Lodekka LD6G	ECW H33/27R	Southern Vectis Omnibus Co	563	R
TDL 998	1960	Bristol Lodekka FS6G	ECW H33/27R	Southern Vectis Omnibus Co *	565	R
YDL 318	1962	Bristol Lodekka FS6G	ECW H33/27R	Southern Vectis Omnibus Co *	573	R
CDL 479C	1965	Bristol Lodekka FLF6G	ECW H38/32F	Southern Vectis Omnibus Co *	611	R
FDL 927D	1966	Bristol MW6G	ECW B43F	Southern Vectis Omnibus Co *	806	R
KDL 885F	1968	Bristol RESH6G	Duple C45F	Southern Vectis Omnibus Co *	301	R
VDL 264K	1972	Bedford YRQ	Plaxton B47F	Seaview Services		A
TDL 126S	1977	Bedford YMT	Duple C51F	Southern Vectis Omnibus Co	126	A
YDL 135T	1979	Ford R1014	Duple B47F	Isle of Wight County Council	5809	A
B259 MDL	1985	Ford Transit 190D	Carlyle B16F	Southern Vectis Omnibus Co	259	A

Notes:

*	Vehicles still owned by Southern Vectis and loaned to museum
AUF 666	Rebodied 1949
MDL 954	Originally H33/27R; converted to open-top in 1973 and renumbered OT4
PDL 519	Originally H33/27R

Above: Keighley Bus Museum is home to former Leeds 139 (ANW 682), a Roe-bodied AEC Regent of 1934 which has recently been returned to working order. In September 1999 the bus revisited old haunts in Leeds on service 50. *Philip Lamb*

Below: The subject of another recent restoration was EVD 406, a 1949 Crossley DD42. New to Baxter's of Airdrie, it spent most of its working life in Yorkshire, being acquired by Wood's of Mirfield in 1953, and was given a new Roe body in 1955. *Philip Lamb*

Contact address: Denholme House Farm, Halifax Road, Denholme, West Yorkshire, BD13 4EN
Phone: 01282 413179 or 01274 587519
Affiliation: NARTM
Brief description: A collection of buses, coaches and ancillary vehicles. Some are owned by the Trust and others by private individuals. The Trust aims to establish a permanent home for the collection in central Keighley.
Events planned: Please see the enthusiast press for details.

Opening days/times: Sundays throughout the year. Tuesdays and Thursdays after 1800. Access at other times by appointment.
Directions by car: Between Keighley and Halifax, at Denholme. The Museum is located behind the Parish Church.
Directions by public transport: Frequent buses from Keighley to Denholme.
Charges: Special events: £2 Adult, £1 concession. Otherwise free but donations welcome.
Facilities: B(e) P T

Registration	Date	Chassis	Body	New to	Fleet No	Status
KW 2260	1927	Leyland Lion PLSC3	Leyland B35R	Bradford Corporation	325	A
TF 6860	1931	Leyland Lion LT3	Leyland B36R	Rawtenstall Corporation	61	RP
ANW 682	1934	AEC Regent I 661	Roe H30/26R	Leeds City Transport	139	R
CWX 671	1938	Bristol K5G	Roe L27/28R	Keighley-West Yorkshire Services	KDG26	R
EUF 198	1938	Leyland Titan TD5	Short	Southdown Motor Services	0198	RP
CFM 354	1938	Leyland Titan TD5	ECW L26/26R	Crosville Motor Services	M52	RP
RN 8622	1939	Leyland Titan TD5	Alexander L27/26R	Ribble Motor Services	2057	R
FWW 596	1947	Bedford OB	Duple C26F	West Yorkshire Road Car Co	646	A
CUH 856	1947	Leyland Tiger PS1	ECW B35R	Western Welsh Omnibus Co	856	A
HOD 30	1948	Bristol L6A	Beadle C31F	Western National Omnibus Co (Royal Blue)	1228	R
MNW 86	1948	Leyland Tiger PS1	Roe B36R	Leeds City Transport	28	R
FWX 914	1948	Sunbeam F4	East Lancs H37/29F	Bradford Corporation	844	R
NNW 492	1949	AEC Regent III 9612E	Roe H31/25R	Leeds City Transport	492	RP
EVD 406	1949	Crossley DD42/7	Roe H31/25R	Baxter's Bus Service, Airdrie	34	RP
NUB 609	1950	AEC Regent III 9612E	(chassis only)	Leeds City Transport	609	A
LYR 533	1951	AEC Regent III O961	Park Royal H30/26R	London Transport	RT3314	R
NHN 128	1951	Bristol LL6B	ECW DP33R	United Automobile Services	BBE1	R
JWU 886	1951	Bristol LL5G	ECW B39R	West Yorkshire Road Car Co	SGL16	R
HKW 82	1952	AEC Regent III 9613E	East Lancs H31/28R	Bradford City Transport	82	R
PJX 43	1952	Leyland Titan PD2/37	Weymann H36/28F	Halifax Corporation	43	RP
LWR 424	1953	Bristol KSW6G	ECW	West Yorkshire Road Car Co	4044	A
AEK 514	1953	Leyland Royal Tiger PSU1/13	Northern Counties B44F	Wigan Corporation	101	A
SVS 904	1954	Bristol LS6G	ECW C35F	Southern National Omnibus Co	1381	R
PGK 872	1955	Bedford SBG	Mulliner B30F	Ministry of Supply		A
UUA 214	1955	Leyland Titan PD2/11	Roe H33/25R	Leeds City Transport	214	RP
XLG 477	1956	Atkinson Alpha PL745H	Northern Counties B34C	SHMD Board	77	RP
VTU 76	1956	Daimler CVG6	Northern Counties H35/23C	SHMD Board	76	RP
GJX 331	1956	Daimler CVG6	Roe H37/26R	Halifax Corporation	119	R
SYG 561	1957	Bedford SBG	Duple C41F	Walton & Helliwell, Mytholmroyd		A
KAG 856	1957	Leyland Titan PD2/20	Alexander L31/28R	Western SMT Co	D1375	RP
DHD 177	1959	AEC Regent V 2LD3RA	Metro-Cammell H39/31F	Yorkshire Woollen District Transport Co	797	A
RCP 237	1962	AEC Regent V 2D3RA	Northern Counties H39/32F	Hebble Motor Services	619	A
PJX 232	1962	Leyland Leopard L1	Weymann B44F	Halifax Joint Omnibus Committee	232	R
RJX 250	1963	Albion Nimbus NS3AN	Weymann DP31F	Halifax Joint Omnibus Committee	250	RP
6220 KW	1964	AEC Regent V 2D3RA	Metro-Cammell H40/30F	Bradford City Transport	220	R
TRN 731	1964	Leyland Leopard PSU3/3R	Plaxton C49F	W. C. Standerwick	731S	R
ENW 980D	1966	AEC Regent V 2D2RA	Roe H39/31R	Leeds City Transport	980	RP
KWT 642D	1966	Bristol Lodekka FS6B	ECW H33/27RD	West Yorkshire Road Car Co	DX210	R
NWU 265D	1966	Bristol Lodekka FS6B	ECW H33/27RD	York-West Yorkshire Joint Committee	YDX221	A
HNW 131D	1966	Daimler Fleetline CRG6LX	Roe H45/33F	Leeds City Transport	131	R
KVH 473E	1967	Daimler Fleetline CRG6LX	Roe H44/31F	Huddersfield Corporation	473	R
TWW 766F	1967	Bristol RELH6G	ECW C47F	West Yorkshire Road Car Co	CRG6	R
YLG 717F	1967	Bristol RESL6G	Northern Counties B43F	SHMD Board	117	A

Registration	Date	Chassis	Body	New to	Fleet No	Status
LAK 309G	1969	Leyland Titan PD3A/12	Alexander H41/29F	Bradford City Transport	309	R
OWY 750K	1972	Bristol RESL6G	ECW B33D	Keighley-West Yorkshire Services	2109	A
XAK 355L	1972	Daimler Fleetline CRL6	Alexander H43/31F	Bradford City Transport	355	RP
WFM 801K	1972	Leyland National 1151/2R/0403	Leyland National B49F	Crosville Motor Services	SNL801	R
OWT 776M	1974	Bristol RELL6G	ECW B53F	West Yorkshire Road Car Co	1403	R
MUA 45P	1976	Bristol LHS6L	ECW DP27F	West Yorkshire PTE	45	A
MUA 870P	1976	Leyland Atlantean AN68/1R	Roe H43/30F	Yorkshire Woollen District Transport Co	773	R

Notes:

TF 6860	Used as a tow bus and snow plough 1950-63
CWX 671	Rebodied 1950
EUF 198	Converted to a towing vehicle from bus 198 in 1957
RN 8622	Chassis refurbished and rebodied in 1949
FWX 914	Trolleybus; rebodied 1963
NNW 492	Leeds City Transport driver trainer 1968-71
EVD 406	New with Scottish Commercial body; acquired by J. Wood & Son, Mirfield, in 1953 and rebodied 1955
LWR 424	Originally bus 858 (later DGW4); converted to a towing vehicle and renumbered 4044 in 1972
SVS 904	Originally registered OTT 90
UUA 214	Leeds City Transport driver trainer 1972-8
KWT 642D	Renumbered 1810 in 1971
NWU 265D	Renumbered 3821 in 1971
TWW 766F	Renumbered 1019 in 1971; restored in later guise as 2508
OWY 750K	Originally B44F
WFM 801K	Second production Leyland National, delivered as B44D; converted to single-door by Greater Manchester Buses (South)
OWT 776M	Delivered with Leyland 680 engine

Above: Resident at Keighley are a number of former Bradford City Transport vehicles. Seen here are 220 (6220 KW), a 1964 AEC Regent V/Metro-Cammell, and 309 (LAK 309G), a 1969 Leyland PD3/Alexander. *Philip Lamb*

Right: As well as having the longest title of any municipal operator, the Stalybridge, Hyde, Mossley & Dukinfield Transport & Electricity Board had a penchant for centre-entrance double-deckers. Northern Counties-bodied Daimler CVG6 No 76 (VTU 76) of 1956 is now on the other side of the Pennines, at Keighley. *Stephen Morris*

Lincolnshire Road Transport Museum   North Hykeham

Contact address: Whisby Road, North Hykeham, Lincoln LN6 3QT
Phone: 01522 689497
Fax: 01522 689292
Website: www.lvvs.freeserve.co.uk
Affiliation: NARTM
Brief description: An impressive collection of over 40 vehicles including classic cars, commercials, buses and motor cycles, mostly with Lincolnshire connections. Fifty years of road transport history is represented in the museum hall, which was built in 1993.
Events planned: Open days on 23 April 2000, 5 Nov 2000
Opening days/times:
May to October: Monday to Friday 12.00 to 16.00; Sunday 10.00 to 16.00;

November to April: Sunday 12.00 to 17.00
Directions by car: Just off A46 Lincoln by-pass on Whisby Road, which links A46 to B1190.
Directions by public transport:
One mile from North Hykeham railway station.
Whisby Road is just off Doddington Road, served by several bus routes.
Charges: No charge but donations welcome.
Facilities: A B(e) D P T
Other information: Refreshments available on open days.

Registration	Date	Chassis	Body	New to	Fleet No	Status
KW 474	1927	Leyland Lion PLSC1	Leyland B31F	Blythe & Berwick, Bradford		R
TE 8318	1929	Chevrolet LQ	Spicer C14D	Jardine, Morcambe		R
WH 1553	1929	Leyland Titan TD1	Leyland L27/24RO	Bolton Corporation	54	R
VL 1263	1929	Leyland Lion LT1	Applewhite B32R	Lincoln Corporation	5	R
TF 818	1930	Leyland Lion LT1	Roe B30F	Lancashire United Transport	202	R
KW 7604	1930	Leyland Badger TA4	Plaxton B20F	Bradford Education Committee	023	R
FW 5698	1935	Leyland Tiger TS7	Burlingham B35F	Lincolnshire Road Car Co	1411	R
RC 2721	1935	SOS DON	Brush B—F	Trent Motor Traction Co	321	R
FHN 833	1940	Bristol L5G	ECW B35F	United Automobile Services	BLO133	RP
BFE 419	1941	Leyland Titan TD7	Roe H30/26R	Lincoln Corporation	64	R
DBE 187	1946	Bristol K6A	ECW H30/26R	Lincolnshire Road Car Co	2115	RP
AHE 163	1946	Leyland Titan PD1	Roe H31/25R	Yorkshire Traction	726	RP
DFE 383	1948	Guy Arab III	Guy H30/26R	Lincoln Corporation	23	R
HPW 133	1949	Bristol K5G	ECW H30/26R	Eastern Counties Omnibus Co	LKH133	R
OHK 432	1949	Daimler CVD6	Roberts H30/26R	Colchester Corporation	4	R
ONO 59	1949	Bristol K5G	ECW L—/—R	Eastern National Omnibus Co	4038	R
FFU 860	1949	AEC Regal III 9621E	Willowbrook DP35F	Enterprise, Scunthorpe	60	R
LTB 907	1950	Bedford OB	Duple C29F	Penn, Warrington		R
FDO 573	1953	AEC Regent III 9613E	Willowbrook H32/28RD	J. W. Camplin & Sons ('Holme Delight'), Donington		R
OLD 714	1954	AEC Regent III O961	Weymann H30/26R	London Transport	RT4494	R
LFW 326	1955	Bristol Lodekka LD6B	ECW H33/25RD	Lincolnshire Road Car Co	2318	R
RFE 416	1961	Leyland Titan PD2/41	Roe H33/28R	Lincoln City Transport	89	R
952 JUB	1964	AEC Regent V 2D2RA	Roe H39/31R	Leeds City Transport	952	R
EVL 549E	1967	Leyland Panther PSUR1/1R	Roe DP45F	Lincoln City Transport	41	RP

Notes:

KW 474	Restored as Lincoln Corporation No 1
FW 5698	Rebodied 1949
DFE 383	Ruston Hornsby air cooled engine
ONO 59	Renumbered 1427 in 1954 and 2255 in 1964; subsequently converted to caravan
FFU 860	Passed to Lincolnshire Road Car Co (860) in 1950

Above: Former Lincoln Corporation Leyland Lion No 5 (VL 1263) dates from 1929; its locally-produced Applewhite body was extensively rebuilt at Lincoln in the mid-1980s. *Stephen Morris*

Below: FFU 860 is a Willowbrook-bodied AEC Regal III, new in 1949 to independent operator Enterprise, Scunthorpe, which was taken over by Lincolnshire Road Car the following year. *David Reed*

London Transport Museum Covent Garden

Contact address: 39 Wellington Street, London WC2E 7BB.
Phone: 0207 379 6344; recorded information 0207 836 8557
E-mail: website: www.ltmuseum.co.uk
Affiliation: NARTM
Brief description: Travel through time at the London Transport Museum. It's London's history. It's London's people. It's trams, trains, buses and more. It's a hands-on moving experience right in the heart of London at Covent Garden.
Opening days/times: Daily 10.00 to 18.00 (Fri 11.00 to 18.00) Last admission 17.15. Closed 24, 25 and 26 December.

Directions by car: Limited parking at parking meters in Holborn/Kingsway area.
Directions by public transport:
Buses to Strand or Aldwych: 1, 4, 6, 9, 11, 13, 15, 23, 26, 68, 76, 77A, 91, 168, 171, 171A, 176, 188, 501, 505 and 521.
Underground to Covent Garden, Leicester Square or Holborn.
Charges: Adult £5.50, Child £2.95, Family £13.95; for school rates please telephone Resource Centre.
Facilities: A C D F G H L R S T

Registration	Date	Chassis	Body	New to	Fleet No	Status
*	1829	Horse bus	LGOC	George Shillibeer		R
–	1875	Horse bus	Thomas Tilling -24-	Thomas Tilling		R
†	1888	Horse bus	LGOC -26-	London General Omnibus Co		R
LC 3701	1906	De Dion	(chassis only)	London General Omnibus Co	L7	R
LA 9928	1911	LGOC B	LGOC O18/16RO	London General Omnibus Co	B340	R
XC 8059	1921	AEC K	LGOC O24/22RO	London General Omnibus Co	K424	R
XM 7399	1923	AEC S	LGOC O28/26RO	London General Omnibus Co	S742	R
MN 2615	1923	Tilling-Stevens TS3A Petrol-Electric	(chassis only)	Douglas Corporation	10	R
YR 3844	1926	AEC NS	LGOC H28/24RO	London General Omnibus Co	NS1995	R
GO 5198	1931	AEC Renown 664	LGOC B—F	London General Omnibus Co	LT1076	RP
GK 3192	1931	AEC Regent 661	LGOC H28/20R	London General Omnibus Co	ST821	R
GK 5323	1931	AEC Renown 663	LGOC H33/23R	London General Omnibus Co	LT165	R
GK 5486	1931	AEC Regal 662	Duple C30F	London General Omnibus Co	T219	R
HX 2756+	1931	AEC 663T	UCC H32/24R	London United Tramways	1	R
AYV 651	1934	AEC Regent 661	LPTB H30/26R	London Transport	STL469	R
BXD 576	1935	AEC Q O762	BRCW B35C	London Transport	Q55	R
CLE 122	1936	Leyland Cub KP03	Weymann B20F	London Transport	C94	RP
EXV 253+	1939	Leyland LPTB70	Leyland H40/30R	London Transport	1253	R
FJJ 774	1939	Leyland Tiger FEC	LPTB B34F	London Transport	TF77	R
HYM 768+	1948	BUT 9641T	Metro-Cammell H40/30R	London Transport	1768	R
NLE 537	1953	AEC Regal IV 9821LT	Metro-Cammell B39F	London Transport	RF537	R
MXX 364	1953	Guy Special NLLVP	ECW B26F	London Transport	GS64	R
NXP 997	1954	AEC Regent III O961	Park Royal H30/26R	London Transport	RT4712	R
OLD 589	1954	AEC Regent III O961	Park Royal H30/26R	London Transport	RT4825	R
SLT 56	1956	AEC Routemaster	Park Royal/LTE H36/28R	London Transport	RM1	R
SLT 57	1957	AEC Routemaster	Park Royal/LTE H36/28R	London Transport	RM2	R
737 DYE	1963	AEC Routemaster 2R2RH	Park Royal H36/28R	London Transport	RM1737	R
CUV 229C	1965	AEC Routemaster R2RH/1	Park Royal H36/29RD	London Transport	RCL2229	R
KGY 4D	1966	AEC Routemaster FR2R	Park Royal H41/31F	London Transport	FRM1	RP
AML 582H	1969	AEC Merlin 4P2R	MCW B25D	London Transport	MBA582	R
EGP 1J	1970	Daimler Fleetline CRG6LXB	Park Royal H44/24D	London Transport	DMS1	R
KJD 401P	1976	Bristol LH6L	ECW B39F	London Transport	BL1	RP
NUW 567Y	1982	Leyland Titan TNLXB/2RR	Leyland H44/24D	London Transport	T567	RP
C526 DYT	1986	Volkswagen LT55	Optare B25F	London Transport	OV2	R
‡	1993	Optare Metrorider	Optare B26F	London Transport	'MRL242'	R

+ Trolleybus

Notes:

*	Unregistered; reconstruction
–	Unregistered
†	Unregistered; 'Garden Seat' type
HYM 768	Trolleybus; on display at East Anglia Transport Museum

‡   Unregistered sectioned exhibit built especially for LT Museum

Right: Now owned by the London Transport Museum, XM 7399 is an AEC S-type new to London General in 1923 as S742, and is one of only a few London buses from this period to survive. *Philip Lamb*

Below: Ancient and modern, seen at the London Transport Museum's Acton depot. GK 3192 is a 1931 AEC Regent new to London General as ST821; nearly 40 years its junior, EGP 1J is a 1970 Daimler Fleetline/Park Royal, new as London Transport DMS1 in 1970. *Philip Lamb*

Above: Seen outside the Manchester Museum of Transport, EDB 562 is an all-Leyland PD2, new as Stockport 308 in 1951. *Philip Lamb*

Right: A vehicle of particular historical significance is TTD 386H, an East Lancs-bodied Leyland PD3 delivered as Ramsbottom 11 in 1969, being the last half-cab double-decker for a British operator. *Stephen Morris*

Manchester Museum of Transport
Cheetham

Contact address: Boyle Street, Cheetham, Manchester M8 8UL
Phone/Fax: 0161 205 2122
Website: www.gmts.co.uk
Affiliation: NARTM
Brief description:
The museum houses over 70 buses and coaches from the Greater Manchester area, from an 1870 horse bus to a 1990 Metrolink tram. Travel back to a time of twopenny singles and coach trips to Blackpool. Extensive displays of photos, uniforms and models complement the vehicles, and visitors may enter many of the vehicles and view the museum's workshop.

Events planned:
25/26 March 2000 — Spring Transport Festival
6/7 May 2000 — 'A Classic Century'
10/11 June 2000 — Accessible Transport Weekend
3 September 2000 — Trans-Lancs rally

Opening days/times: Wednesdays, Saturdays, Sundays & Bank Holidays: 10.00 to 17.00 (please 'phone for Christmas/New Year opening)
Directions by car:
From M62/M60 junction 18, follow 'Castlefields' signs to Cheetham Hill; from City, follow A665 (Cheetham Hill Road) — Museum signposted.
Directions by public transport:
Bus 135 or 59 to Queen's Road; Metrolink tram to Woodlands Road (10min walk)
Charges: £2.50 adult, £1.50 concession, £7 family. Season ticket available.
Facilities: B(e) C D F G H P R S T
Other information: Archives available for study by arrangement.

Registration	Date	Chassis	Body	New to	Fleet No	Status
*	1890	Horse bus	Manchester Carriage Co O—/—RO	Manchester Carriage Co	2	R
DB 5070	1925	Tilling-Stevens TS6	Brush O54RO	North Western Road Car Co	170	R
CK 3825	1927	Leyland Lion PLSC1	Leyland B31F	Ribble Motor Services	295	R
VM 4439	1928	Leyland Tiger TS1	Metro-Cammell/Crossley B32R	Manchester Corporation	138	A

Registration	Date	Chassis	Body	New to	Fleet No	Status
VY 957	1929	Leyland Lion PLSC1	Ribble B32R	York Corporation	2	R
VR 5742	1930	Leyland Tiger TS2	Manchester Corporation Car Works B30R	Manchester Corporation	28	R
AXJ 857	1934	Leyland Titan TD3	(chassis only)	Manchester Corporation	526	R
JA 7585	1935	Leyland Tiger TS7	English Electric B35C	Stockport Corporation	185	A
RN 7824	1936	Leyland Cheetah LZ2	Brush C31F	Ribble Motor Services	1568	RP
EFJ 92	1938	Bedford WTB	Heaver C25F	Taylor, Exeter	-	RP
BBA 560	1939	AEC Regent O661	Park Royal H26/22R	Salford Corporation	235	RP
AJA 152	1939	Bristol K5G	Willowbrook L27/26R	North Western Road Car Co	432	R
JP 4712	1940	Leyland Titan TD7	Leyland L27/26R	Wigan Corporation	70	RP
BJA 425	1946	Bristol L5G	Willowbrook B38R	North Western Road Car Co	270	R
HTB 656	1946	Leyland Tiger PS1	Roe B35R	Ramsbottom Corporation	17	R
HTF 586	1947	Bedford OB	SMT C29F	Warburton Bros, Bury		R
CDB 224	1948	Leyland Titan PD2/1	Leyland L27/26R	North Western Road Car Co	224	R
CWH 717	1948	Leyland Titan PD2/4	Leyland	Bolton Corporation	367	R
JND 791	1948	Crossley DD42/8S	Crossley H32/26R	Manchester Corporation	2150	R
JNA 467	1949	Leyland Titan PD1/3	Metro-Cammell H32/26R	Manchester Corporation	3166	RP
LMA 284	1949	Foden PVSC6	Lawton C35F	R. Bullock & Co, Cheadle		R
BEN 177	1950	AEC Regent III 9613A	Weymann H30/26R	Bury Corporation	177	R
LTC 774+	1950	Crossley Empire TDD42/2	Crossley H30/26R	Ashton-under-Lyne Corporation	80	RP
CWG 206	1950	Leyland Tiger PS1	Alexander C35F	W. Alexander & Sons	PA164	R
MTB 848	1950	Leyland Tiger PS2/1	East Lancs B35R	Rawtenstall Corporation	55	RP
HDK 835	1951	AEC Regent III 9612E	East Lancs H31/26R	Rochdale Corporation	235	RP
JND 646	1951	Leyland Titan PD2/3	Metro-Cammell H32/26R	Manchester Corporation	3245	R
JVU 775+	1951	Crossley Dominion TDD64/1	Crossley H36/30R	Manchester Corporation	1250	R
EDB 549	1951	Leyland Titan PD2/1	Leyland O28/20R	Stockport Corporation	295	R
EDB 562	1951	Leyland Titan PD2/1	Leyland H30/26R	Stockport Corporation	308	R
EDB 575	1951	Crossley DD42/7	Crossley H30/26R	Stockport Corporation	321	R
NNB 125	1953	Leyland Royal Tiger PSU1/13	Northern Counties B41C	Manchester Corporation	25	R
UTC 672	1954	AEC Regent III 9613S	East Lancs L27/28RD	Bamber Bridge Motor Services	4	R
UMA 370	1955	Atkinson PD746	Northern Counties H35/24C	SHMD Board	70	R
NDK 980	1956	AEC Regent V D2RA6G	Weymann H33/28R	Rochdale Corporation	280	R
JBN 153	1956	Leyland Titan PD2/13	Metro-Cammell H34/28R	Bolton Corporation	77	R
PND 460	1956	Leyland Titan PD2/12	Metro-Cammell H36/28R	Manchester Corporation	3460	R
DJP 754	1957	Leyland Titan PD2/30	Northern Counties H33/28R	Wigan Corporation	115	R
NBU 494	1957	Leyland Titan PD2/20	Roe H31/29R	Oldham Corporation	394	R
116 JTD	1958	Guy Arab IV	Northern Counties H41/32R	Lancashire United Transport	21	R
122 JTD	1958	Guy Arab IV	Northern Counties H41/32R	Lancashire United Transport	27	R
TNA 496	1958	Leyland Titan PD2/40	Burlingham H37/28R	Manchester Corporation	3496	R
TNA 520	1958	Leyland Titan PD2/34	Burlingham H37/28R	Manchester Corporation	3520	R
YDK 590	1960	AEC Reliance 2MU3RA	Harrington C37F	Yelloway Motor Services, Rochdale		R
HEK 705	1961	Leyland Titan PD3A/2	Massey H41/29F	Wigan Corporation	57	R
TRJ 112	1962	Daimler CVG6	Metro-Cammell H37/28R	Salford City Transport	112	RP
414 CLT	1963	AEC Routemaster 2R2RH	Park Royal H36/28R	London Transport	RM1414	R
4632 VM	1963	Daimler CVG6K	Metro-Cammell H37/28R	Manchester Corporation	4632	R
REN 116	1963	Leyland Atlantean PDR1/1	Metro-Cammell H41/33F	Bury Corporation	116	RP
8860 VR	1964	AEC Regent V 2D3RA	East Lancs H41/32R	A. Mayne & Son, Manchester		R
PTC 114C	1965	AEC Renown 3B3RA	East Lancs H41/31F	Leigh Corporation	15	R
DDB 174C	1965	Daimler Fleetline CRG6LX	Alexander H44/31F	North Western Road Car Co	174	R
PTE 944C	1965	Leyland Titan PD2/37	Roe H37/28F	Ashton-under-Lyne Corporation	44	R
DBA 214C	1965	Leyland Atlantean PDR1/1	Metro-Cammell H43/33F	Salford City Transport	214	RP
BND 874C	1965	Leyland Panther Cub PSURC1/1	Park Royal B43D	Manchester Corporation	74	RP
FRJ 254D	1966	Leyland Titan PD2/40	MCW H36/28F	Salford City Transport	254	R
JRJ 281E	1967	Leyland Titan PD2/40	MCW H36/28F	Salford City Transport	281	R
HVM 901F	1968	Leyland Atlantean PDR1/1	Park Royal H45/28D	Manchester City Transport	1001	R
KDB 408F	1968	Leyland Leopard PSU4/1R	East Lancs B43D	Stockport Corporation	408	RP
KJA 871F	1968	Leyland Titan PD3/14	East Lancs H38/32R	Stockport Corporation	71	R
MJA 891G	1969	Leyland Titan PD3/14	East Lancs H38/32R	Stockport Corporation	91	R
MJA 897G	1969	Leyland Titan PD3/14	East Lancs O38/32F	Stockport Corporation	97	R
TTD 386H	1969	Leyland Titan PD3/14	East Lancs H41/32F	Ramsbottom Corporation	11	R

Registration	Date	Chassis	Body	New to	Fleet No	Status
TXJ 507K	1972	Leyland National 1151/2R/0202	Leyland National B46D	SELNEC PTE	EX30	R
VNB 101L	1972	Leyland Atlantean AN68/1R	Park Royal H43/32F	SELNEC PTE	7001	R
XVU 352M	1974	Seddon Pennine IV-236	Seddon B19F	Greater Manchester PTE	1722	A
GNC 276N	1975	Seddon-Lucas	Seddon B19F	Greater Manchester PTE	EX62	R
HVU 244N	1975	AEC Reliance 6U3ZR	Plaxton C49F	Yelloway Motor Services, Rochdale		R
ORJ 83W	1981	MCW Metrobus DR102/21	MCW H43/30F	Greater Manchester PTE	5083	A
A706 LNC	1984	Leyland Atlantean AN68D/1R	Northern Counties H43/32F	Greater Manchester PTE	8706	R
D63 NOF	1986	Freight Rover Sherpa 365	Carlyle B18F	Manchester Minibuses ('Bee Line Buzz Co')		A

+ Trolleybus

Notes:

*	Largest surviving horse bus
DB 5070	Petrol-electric transmission
CK 3825	Body rebuilt 1981
VM 4439	Body new 1935
VY 957	Body rebuilt 1983; restored in Ribble livery
VR 5742	Rebodied 1937
AJA 152	Rebodied 1951
BJA 425	Originally numbered 125; rebodied 1952
CWH 717	Originally H30/26R; converted to tower wagon
LMA 284	Body new 1954
EDB 549	Originally H30/26R
UMA 370	Only Atkinson double-decker bodied
414 CLT	Loaned to Manchester Corporation when new
HVM 901F	First 'Mancunian' double-decker
MJA 891G	Last open-rear-platform double-decker delivered to a British operator
MJA 897G	Originally H38/32F; converted to open-top in 1982

TTD 386H	Last half-cab double-decker delivered to a British operator
TXJ 507K	First production Leyland National
VNB 101L	First SELNEC Standard double-decker
GNC 276N	Battery-powered

Right: One of the latest arrivals at the Manchester Museum of Transport is ORJ 83W, a 1981 MCW Metrobus new as Greater Manchester 5083. Donated by First Manchester, it is currently in that operator's all-over orange livery.
Philip Lamb

Above: PDU 125M is a former Coventry Daimler Fleetline/East Lancs, preserved in the city where its chassis was built in 1973. Converted to open-top following withdrawal by West Midlands, it still carries the livery applied to celebrate Coventry City's FA Cup victory in 1987. *Philip Lamb*

Museum of British Road Transport   Coventry

Contact address: Hales Street, Coventry CV1 1PN
Phone: 024 7683 2425
Fax: 024 7683 2465
E-mail: museum@mbrt.co.uk
Brief description: The museum has over 210 cars and commercial vehicles, over 90 motorcycles and around 240 bicycles. Various tableaux chart the development of the motor vehicle from the early years, and Coventry's contribution to this can be seen in the many marques on display. Other exhibits include a 633mph land speed record car, several thousand die-cast models and a walk through audio visual display of the Coventry Blitz experience.

Events planned: Please see the enthusiast press for details.
Opening days/times: Seven days a week, 10.00 to 17.00 (except Christmas Eve, Christmas Day and Boxing Day.)
Directions by car: Follow brown 'Motor Museum' signs from Coventry City Centre.
Directions by public transport: Museum is close to Pool Meadow bus station; use bus 17 or 27 from Coventry railway station to Pool Meadow.
Charges: Free admission
Facilities: A D F G H L R S T

Registration	Date	Chassis	Body	New to	Fleet No	Status
EKV 966	1944	Daimler CWA6	Roe H31/25R	Coventry Corporation	366	R
JNB 416	1948	Maudslay Marathon II	Trans-United C33F	Hackett's, Manchester		R
KOM 150	1950	Daimler CVD6	Wilsdon (mobile press)	Birmingham Post & Mail		R
SRB 424	1953	Daimler CD650	Willowbrook L27/28RD	Tailby & George ('Blue Bus Services'), Willington		R
PBC 734	1956	Karrier Bantam Q25	Reading C14F	Mablethorpe Homes, Leicester		R
333 CRW	1963	Daimler CVG6	Metro-Cammell H34/29R	Coventry Corporation	333	R
PDU 125M	1973	Daimler Fleetline CRG6LX	East Lancs O44/30F	Coventry Corporation	125	R

Notes:

EKV 966	Rebodied 1951; converted to mobile repair workshop (02) in 1960	PBC 734	Welfare bus
KOM 150	Currently used as museum promotional vehicle	PDU 125M	Originally H44/30F; converted to open-top in 1986

Museum of Transport   Glasgow

Contact address: Kelvin Hall, 1 Bunhouse Road, Glasgow G3 8DP
Phone: 0141 287 2720 (school bookings on 0141 287 2747)
Fax: 0141 287 2692
Affiliation: NARTM
Brief description: The museum displays many items of transport history dating from the 1870s.
Opening days/times: Monday to Saturday, 10.00 to 17.00; Sunday 11.00 to 17.00 (closed 25/26 December and 1/2 January)

Directions by car: From M8 junctions 17 or 19
Directions by public transport: Bus from City Centre (Dumbarton Road) to Kelvin Hall; Underground to Kelvin Hall; nearest main-line railway station is Partick.
Charges: Free admission
Facilities: D F G H R T
Other information: Guided tours and exhibitions also held.

Registration	Date	Chassis	Body	New to	Fleet No	Status
EGA 79	1949	Albion Venturer CX37S	Croft H30/26R	Glasgow Corporation	B92	R
FYS 988	1958	BUT RETB1	Burlingham B50F	Glasgow Corporation	TBS13	R
FYS 998	1958	Leyland Atlantean PDR1/1	Alexander H44/34F	Glasgow Corporation	LA1	R

Notes:
FYS 988   Trolleybus; exhibited at the 1958 Commercial Motor Show

National Museum of Science and Industry   Wroughton

Contact address: Exhibition Road, London SW7 2DD
Phone: 0207 942 4209
E-mail: k.shirt@nmsi.ac.uk
Brief description: The bus collection is located at Wroughton, near Swindon, Wiltshire.
Events planned: Open days are held and details of these may be found in the enthusiast press.

Opening days/times: Open only on Transport Festival and Open Days.
Directions by car: On A4361 approx 4 miles south of Swindon.
Directions by public transport: Publicised for Open Days
Charges: Published for each event.
Facilities: n/a

Registration	Date	Chassis	Body	New to	Fleet No	Status
LMJ 653G	1913	Fiat 52B	(unknown)	(operator unknown), Yugoslavia		RP
JCP 60F	1928	Leyland Lion PLSC1	Leyland B31F	Jersey Railways & Tramways		A
DR 4902	1929	Leyland Titan TD1	Leyland L51RO	National Omnibus & Transport Co	2849	A
DX 8871+	1930	Ransomes, Simms & Jefferies D	Ransomes, Simms & Jefferies B31D	Ipswich Corporation	44	A
VO 6806	1931	AEC Regal 662	Cravens B32F	Red Bus, Mansfield		A
GW 713	1931	Gilford 1680T	Weymann C30D	Valliant, Ealing		A
JN 5783	1935	AEC Q 762	(chassis only)	Westcliff-on-Sea Motor Services		A
CPM 61+	1939	AEC 661T	Weymann H28/26R	Brighton, Hove & District Omnibus Co	6340	A
HVF 455L	1940	Saurer CRD	(unknown) C12F	GFM (Switzerland)	52	A
DHR 192	1943	Guy Arab II	Weymann H30/26R	Swindon Corporation	51	A
KPT 909	1949	Leyland Titan PD2/1	Leyland L27/26R	Weardale Motor Services, Frosterley		R
LTA 772	1951	Bristol LWL5G	ECW B32R	Western National Omnibus Co	1613	A
NLP 645	1953	AEC Regal IV 9822E	Park Royal RDP37C	British European Airways	1035	A
OTT 55	1953	Bristol LS5G	ECW B41F	Southern National Omnibus Co	1701	A
HET 513	1953	Crossley DD42/8	Crossley H30/26R	Rotherham Corporation	213	A
OLJ 291	1954	Bedford CAV	Bedford B12	(non-psv use)		A
VLT 140	1960	AEC Routemaster R2RH	Park Royal H36/28R	London Transport	RM140	R
504 EBL	1963	Bedford VAL14	Duple C52F	Reliance Motor Services, Newbury	87	A
*	1970	Moulton MD	Moulton C23F	Moulton development vehicle		A
BCD 820L	1973	Leyland National 1151/1R/0102	Leyland National B49F	Southdown Motor Services	20	A
+ Trolleybus						

Notes:

JCP 60F	Originally registered J 4601
HVF455L	Displays original, Swiss registration FR 1347
*	Eight-wheeled integral development vehicle (unregistered)

Left: Former Southern National ECW-bodied LS 1701 (OTT 55) of 1953 passed to Western National when the two companies merged in 1969, and went on to become the last bus of its type in service with a National Bus Company subsidiary. It is now preserved by the Science Museum at Wroughton, near Swindon. *Stephen Morris*

Above right: 504 EBL is currently the only restored example of a Duple Vega Major-bodied Bedford VAL, and was formerly No 87 in the fleet of Reliance, Newbury. It is seen here next to former Southdown Leyland National No 20 (BCD 820L), surrounded by earlier forms of transport at the Science Museum's annexe near Swindon. *Stephen Morris*

North of England Open Air Museum   Beamish

Contact address: Beamish, Co Durham, DH9 0RG
Phone: 01207 231811
Fax: 01207 290933
E-mail: Beamish@neoam.demon.co.uk
Brief description: Beamish is an open-air museum which vividly recreates life in the North of England in the 19th and early 20th century. Buildings from throughout the region have been brought to Beamish, rebuilt and furnished as they once were. Costumed staff welcome visitors and demonstrate the past way of life in The Town, Colliery Village, Home Farm, Railway Station, Pockerley Manor and 1825 Railway. A one-mile circular period tramway carries visitors around the Museum and a replica 1913 Daimler bus operates between The Town and Colliery Village.
Events planned:
21 to 24 April 2000 — The History of Meccano
11 June 2000 — Morgan car meeting
2/3 September 2000 — Vintage collections weekend
24 Sept 2000 — Classic car day

Opening days/times:
April to October: 10.00 to 17.00 (open every day)
November to April: 10.00 to 16.00 (closed Mondays and Fridays); closed 18 December to 1 January (inclusive)
Directions by car: Follow A1(M) to junction 63 (Chester-le-Street exit). Take A693 towards Stanley and follow Beamish Museum signs.
Directions by public transport: Buses 709 from Newcastle, 720 from Durham and 775/778 from Sunderland all serve Beamish.
Charges:
Summer: Adult £10, Child £6, Over 60s £7.
Winter: £3 per person.
Group rates available for parties of 20 or more.
Facilities: B E F G H M P R T
Other information: Beamish is not ideal for wheelchair users. Free leaflet available in advance for visitors with disabilities and mobility limitations.

Registration	Date	Chassis	Body	New to	Fleet No	Status
WT 7108+	1924	Straker-Clough	Brush B32F	Keighley Corporation	12	A
UP 551	1928	SOS QL	Brush B37F	Northern General Transport Co	338	RP
VK 5401	1931	Dodge UF30A	Robson B14F	Baty, Rookhope		A
LTN 501+	1948	Sunbeam S7	Northern Coachbuilders H39/31R	Newcastle Corporation	501	R
J 2503 + Trolleybus	1988	Renault	Osborne O18/14RO	North of England Open Air Museum		R

Notes:
J 2503   Replica of 1913 Daimler

Contact address: Mere Way, Ruddington, Nottingham NG11 6NX
Phone: 0115 940 5705
E-mail: aecley@aol.co
Affiliation: NARTM
Brief description: The centre offers exhibits covering road and rail transport along with steam road vehicles, and provides the opportunity to experience travel of a bygone age.
Events planned: Please see enthusiast press for details.

Opening days/times: Easter to mid-October: Sundays and Bank Holiday Mondays.
Directions by car: 3 miles south of Nottingham just off A52 ring-road and main A60 road via small roundabout at Ruddington.
Directions by public transport: Buses from Nottingham pass near museum
Charges: Not finalised at time of publication.
Facilities: B B(e) D E G H P R S T

Registration	Date	Chassis	Body	New to	Fleet No	Status
W 963	1923	Daimler CJA	Barton Ch22	Barton Transport, Chilwell		R
VO 8846	1932	Leyland Lion LT5	Willowbrook DP32F	South Notts Bus Co, Gotham	17	A
DJF 349	1947	Leyland Titan PD1	Leyland H30/26R	Leicester City Transport	248	A
CRR 819	1947	Leyland Cub KPZ2	Brush C20F	Barton Transport, Chilwell	284	RP
JVO 230	1948	Leyland Titan PD1A	Duple L29/26F	Barton Transport, Chilwell	507	R
JRR 930	1948	Leyland Titan PD1A	Duple L29/26F	Barton Transport, Chilwell	509	A
MAL 310	1951	Leyland Royal Tiger PSU1/11	Duple DP45F	South Notts Bus Co, Gotham	42	A
OTV 161	1953	AEC Regent III 9613E	Park Royal H30/26R	Nottingham City Transport	161	R
APR 167A	1953	Leyland Titan PD2/12	Leyland H—/—RD	Barton Transport, Chilwell	732	R
NNN 968	1953	Leyland BTS1	Barton C39F	Barton Transport, Chilwell	668	A
VLT 108	1959	AEC Routemaster R2RH	Park Royal H36/28R	London Transport	RM108	R
851 FNN	1960	AEC Regent V 2D3RA	Northern Counties FL37/33F	Barton Transport, Chilwell	851	R
AAL 522A	1960	AEC Regent V 2D3RA	Northern Counties FL37/33F	Barton Transport, Chilwell	854	A
861 HAL	1960	Dennis Loline II	Northern Counties FL37/31F	Barton Transport, Chilwell	861	R
80 NVO	1962	Leyland Titan PD3/4	Northern Counties L33/32F	South Notts Bus Co, Gotham	80	A
YRC 194	1962	Leyland Tiger Cub PSUC1/1	Alexander DP41F	Trent Motor Traction Co	194	RP
RRN 428	1962	Leyland Atlantean PDR1/1	Northern Counties CH39/20F	Ribble Motor Services	1279	A
484 EFJ	1962	Leyland Titan PD2A/30	Metro-Cammell H31/26R	Exeter Corporation	84	A
DAU 370C	1965	AEC Renown 3B3RA	Weymann H40/30F	Nottingham City Transport	370	R
ETO 452C	1965	Leyland Atlantean PDR1/1	Metro-Cammell H—/—F	Nottingham City Transport	452	A
EOD 524D	1966	AEC Regent V 2D3RA	MCW H34/25F	Devon General Omnibus & Touring Co	524	R
FEL 751D	1966	Bristol MW6G	ECW C39F	Hants & Dorset Motor Services	904	R
LNN 89E	1967	Albion Lowlander LR3	Northern Counties H41/30F	South Notts Bus Co, Gotham	89	A
SLK 737F	1968	Bedford J2SZ2	Willowbrook B20F	London Borough of Hackney		R
RCH 518F	1968	Daimler Fleetline CRG6LX	Alexander H44/33F	Trent Motor Traction Co	518	A
STO 523H	1970	Leyland Atlantean PDR1A/1	Northern Counties H47/30D	Nottingham City Transport	523	R
KVO 429P	1975	Leyland National 11351/2R	Leyland National B50F	Trent Motor Traction Co	429	A
ORC 545P	1976	Leyland Atlantean AN68/1R	ECW O—/—F	Northern General Transport Co	3299	R
GTX 761W	1980	Bristol LHS6L	ECW DP27F	National Welsh Omnibus Services	MD8026	RP
VRC 612Y	1982	Leyland Leopard PSU3G/4R	Plaxton C53F	Barton Transport, Chilwell	612	R

Notes:

APR 167A	Originally registered RAL 334
AAL 522A	Originally registered 854 FNN
861 HAL	Carries ultra-low-height (12ft 6in) body
LNN 89E	Last Albion Lowlander delivered; badged 'Leyland'
KVO 429P	Originally B44D
ORC 545P	Originally H45/27D and registered MPT 299P; used as promotional vehicle

Above right: At 12ft 5½in, 861 HAL is the lowest British double-decker ever built. New to Barton as 861 in 1960, it combines an already low-framed Dennis Loline chassis with a lowbridge Northern Counties body. The bus is now resident at the Nottingham Transport Heritage Centre. *Philip Lamb*

Right: Former South Notts 89 (LNN 89E) has the last Albion Lowlander chassis built; bodied by Northern Counties, it was delivered in 1967. The bus now awaits restoration at Ruddington. *Philip Lamb*

Contact address: Station Yard, Long Hanborough, Witney, Oxfordshire, OX8 8LA
Phone: 01993 883617 (Sundays) or 01865 400002
Affiliation: NARTM
Brief description: Over 50 buses dating from 1915 to 1986, mainly from City of Oxford Motor Services and other local companies. The collection includes many vehicles of AEC manufacture.
Events planned: Please see enthusiast press for details.
Opening days/times: Saturdays, Sundays and Bank Holidays, 10.30 to 16.30 (closed Christmas Day)

Directions by car: The entrance is on the south side of the A4095 (Witney-Bicester), between the villages of Bladon and Long Hanborough.
Directions by public transport: Museum is adjacent to Hanborough railway station on the Oxford-Worcester line (journey time 10min from Oxford)
Charges: Adults £3, Children/OAP £1.50, Family £7.
Facilities: B(e) D P R S T
Other information: School parties welcome by arrangement — please telephone in advance.

Registration	Date	Chassis	Body	New to	Fleet No	Status
DU 4838	1915	Daimler Y	City of Oxford Electric Tramways B32R	City of Oxford Electric Tramways	39	RP
*	1916	Daimler Y	(chassis only)			A
*	1916	Daimler Y	(chassis only)			A
FC 2602	1917	Daimler Y	O18/16RO	City of Oxford Electric Tramways	46	A
J 1418	1932	AEC Regal 642	(lorry)	City of Oxford Motor Services	GC41	A
JO 5403	1932	AEC Regent 661	Brush O28/24R	City of Oxford Motor Services	GA16	RP
HA 8047	1933	SOS REDD	Metro-Cammell H26/26R	BMMO ('Midland Red')	1047	RP
FL-14-86	1948	AEC Regal III 9613E	Weymann/CCFL B16D	Carris, Lisbon	123	A
NJO 703	1949	AEC Regal III 9621A	Willowbrook DP32F	City of Oxford Motor Services	703	R
OFC 205	1949	AEC Regal III 6821A	Duple C32F	South Midland Motor Services	66	A
OFC 393	1949	AEC Regent III 9612A	Weymann H30/26R	City of Oxford Motor Services	H892	A
OJO 727	1950	AEC Regal III 9621A	Willowbrook B32F	City of Oxford Motor Services	727	R
PWL 413	1950	AEC Regent III 9613A	Weymann L27/26R	City of Oxford Motor Services	L166	RP
SFC 610	1952	AEC Regal IV 9821S	Willowbrook C37C	City of Oxford Motor Services	610	RP
GJB 254	1952	Bristol LWL6B	ECW B39R	Thames Valley Traction Co	616	A
TWL 928	1953	AEC Regent III 9613S	Park Royal H30/26R	City of Oxford Motor Services	H928	RP
191 AWL	1956	AEC Regent V MD3RV	Weymann L30/26R	City of Oxford Motor Services	L191	R
194 BFC	1957	AEC Regent V MD3RV	Weymann L30/28RD	City of Oxford Motor Services	L194	RP
956 AJO	1957	AEC Regent V MD3RV	Park Royal H33/28R	City of Oxford Motor Services	H956	R
975 CWL	1958	AEC Regent V LD3RA	Park Royal H37/28R	City of Oxford Motor Services	H975	RP
YNX 478	1958	AEC Reliance MU3RA	Duple (Midland) B44F	Chiltern Queens, Woodcote		RP
756 KFC	1960	AEC Reliance 2MU3RV	Park Royal B44F	City of Oxford Motor Services	756	R
304 KFC	1961	Dennis Loline II	East Lancs H35/28F	City of Oxford Motor Services	304	RP
305 KFC	1961	Dennis Loline II	East Lancs H35/28F	City of Oxford Motor Services	305	R
312 MFC	1961	AEC Bridgemaster 2B3RA	Park Royal H43/29F	City of Oxford Motor Services	312	RP
14 LFC	1961	Morris FF	Wadham C27F	Morris Motors, Cowley		A
850 ABK	1962	AEC Reliance 2MU3RA	Duple C43F	Don Motor Coach Co, Southsea		RP
324 NJO	1962	AEC Bridgemaster 2B3RA	Park Royal H40/25F	City of Oxford Motor Services	324	RP
332 RJO	1963	AEC Renown 3B3RA	Park Royal H38/27F	City of Oxford Motor Services	332	RP
340 TJO	1964	AEC Renown 3B3RA	Park Royal H38/27F	City of Oxford Motor Services	340	A
DFC 360D	1966	AEC Renown 3B3RA	(chassis only)	City of Oxford Motor Services	360	R
AD 7156	1966	AEC Renown 2D2RA	Metal Sections H51/39D	Kowloon Motor Bus	A165	A
FWL 371E	1967	AEC Renown 3B3RA	Northern Counties H38/27F	City of Oxford Motor Services	371	RP
NAC 416F	1967	Leyland Atlantean PDR1/1	Northern Counties H44/31F	Stratford-upon-Avon Blue Motors	10	RP
OFC 902H	1970	Bristol VRTSL6LX	ECW H39/31F	City of Oxford Motor Services	902	RP
TJO 56K	1971	AEC Reliance 6MU4R	Marshall DP49F	City of Oxford Motor Services	56	A
UFC 430K	1971	Daimler Fleetline CRL6	Northern Counties H43/27D	City of Oxford Motor Services	430	A
AUD 310J	1971	Leyland Leopard PSU3B/4R	Plaxton C51F	O. A. Slatter & Sons, Long Hanborough	40	A
EUD 256K	1972	AEC Reliance 6MU4R	Plaxton B47F	Chiltern Queens, Woodcote		A
YWL 134K	1972	Leyland Leopard PSU3B/4R	Plaxton C53F	R. Jarvis & Sons, Middle Barton		A
NUD 105L	1973	Bristol VRTSL6LX	ECW CH41/27F	City of Oxford Motor Services	105	A
RBW 87M	1974	Bristol RELH6L	ECW DP49F	City of Oxford Motor Services	87	A
HUD 476S	1977	Bristol VRTSL3/6LXB	ECW H43/27D	City of Oxford Motor Services	476	R

Registration	Date	Chassis	Body	New to	Fleet No	Status
PWL 999W	1980	Leyland Olympian B45/TL11/2R	Alexander H50/32D	Leyland demonstrator		A
UKE 830X	1982	Leyland Leopard PSU3G/4R	ECW C49F	East Kent Road Car Co	8830	A
VUD 30X	1982	Leyland Leopard PSU3G/4R	ECW C49F	City of Oxford Motor Services	30	A
VJO 201X	1982	Leyland Olympian ONLXB/1R	ECW H45/27D	City of Oxford Motor Services	201	A
A869 SUL	1983	Leyland Titan TNLXB/2RRSp	Leyland H44/26D	London Transport	T869	A
B106 XJO	1985	Ford Transit 160D	Dormobile B16F	South Midland	6	A
C729 JJO	1986	Ford Transit 190D	Carlyle DP20F	City of Oxford Motor Services	729	RP

Notes:

DU 4838	Body new 1920
*	Chassis only
FC 2602	Body ex-London built 1906
J 1418	Originally registered JO 5032; passed to Mascot Motors, Jersey, and subsequently converted to lorry
JO 5403	Originally H28/24R
HA 8047	Sole surviving SOS double-decker
FL-14-86	Portuguese registration
YNX 478	Carries 1956 body transferred from Dennis Pelican chassis
305 KFC	Sectioned museum display, showing body construction method
14 LFC	Originally used for Morris Motors band

850 ABK	Acquired by Chiltern Queens, Woodcote, in 1964
DFC 360D	Museum display, showing disposition of chassis units
AD 7156	Hong Kong registration
NAC 416F	Acquired by City of Oxford Motor Services (905) in 1970
PWL 999W	Leyland Olympian prototype built as Far East demonstrator and operated by Singapore Bus Services registered SBS 5396B; later fitted with Gardner engine and acquired by City of Oxford Motor Services (999) in 1987
A869 SUL	Acquired by City of Oxford Motor Services (975) in 1993

Above: For many years, City of Oxford standardised on AEC models — indeed, by 1961 the fleet was 100% AEC — and this domination is reflected in the Oxford Bus Museum's collection. Seen here are L191 (191 AWL), a lowbridge Weymann-bodied Regent V of 1956, and H956 (956 AJO), a highbridge Park Royal-bodied example of 1957; both have exposed radiators, an uncommon feature on the Regent V.

On the right of the picture is another vehicle with Oxford connections — a Cowley-built Morris Minor.
Philip Lamb

Above: Nowadays a resident of the St Helens Transport Museum, former Leigh 16 (KTD 768) is a 1950 Leyland PD2 with rare Lydney lowbridge bodywork. *Philip Lamb*

Below: AEC Reliance/Plaxton bus 453 AUP was new in 1958 as No 53 in the fleet of Co Durham independent Wilkinson's of Sedgefield, and with the company was later taken over by United; it is seen here next to former Lancashire United Guy Arab/Northern Counties 110 (574 TD) of 1962. Both vehicles are cared for by the St Helens Transport Museum. *Stephen Morris*

St Helens Transport Museum

Contact address: The Old Bus Depot, 51 Hall Street, St Helens, WA10 1DU
Phone: 01744 451681
E-mail: E-mail@sthelens-transport-museum.co.uk
Website: www.sthelens-transport-museum.co.uk
Affiliation: NARTM
Brief description: A collection of over 100 historic vehicles representing the transport heritage of the northwest of England. There

is also a small exhibits section containing ticket machines, uniforms, signs and other transport-related items.
Events planned: Please see the enthusiast press for details
Opening days/times: Currently closed pending roof repairs; reopening will be publicised in the enthusiast press and on the St Helens website.
Facilities: A B(e) D G T

Registration	Date	Chassis	Body	New to	Fleet No	Status
ED 6141	1930	Leyland Titan TD1	Massey H28/26R	Warrington Corporation	22	A
KR 1728	1930	Leyland Titan TD1	Short H—/—R	Maidstone & District Motor Services	321	A
KJ 2578	1931	Leyland Titan TD1	Weymann B—C	Redcar Motor Services, Tunbridge Wells		A
AFY 971	1934	Leyland Titan TD3	English Electric O26/25R	Southport Corporation	43	A
RV 6360	1935	Leyland Titan TD4	English Electric O26/24R	Portsmouth Corporation	117	A
FV 6128	1935	Leyland Lion LT7	Burlingham FOB32C	Blackpool Corporation	118	RP
ATD 683	1935	Leyland Lion LT7	Massey B30R	Widnes Corporation	39	R
FTB 11	1941	Leyland Titan TD7	Northern Coachbuilders L27/26R	Leigh Corporation	84	A
EWM 358	1945	Daimler CWA6	Duple H30/26R	Southport Corporation	62	A
DKY 713+	1945	Karrier W	East Lancs H37/29F	Bradford Corporation	713	A
ARN 392	1946	Leyland Titan PD1A	Leyland H30/26R	Preston Corporation	88	RP
DED 797	1946	Leyland Titan PD1	Alexander H30/26R	Warrington Corporation	16	RP
EED 8	1947	Leyland Titan PD1	Alexander H30/26R	Warrington Corporation	24	R
DBU 246	1947	Leyland Titan PD1/3	Roe H31/25R	Oldham Corporation	246	R
FFY 401	1947	Leyland Titan PD2/3	Leyland O30/26R	Southport Corporation	84	A
FFY 403	1947	Leyland Titan PD2/3	Leyland O30/26R	Southport Corporation	86	A
FFY 404	1947	Leyland Titan PD2/3	Leyland O30/26R	Southport Corporation	87	R
HLW 159	1947	AEC Regent III O961	Park Royal H30/26R	London Transport	RT172	R
ACB 902	1947	Guy Arab II	Northern Coachbuilders H30/26R	Blackburn Corporation	74	RP
BCB 341	1948	Leyland Tiger PS1	Crossley B32F	Blackburn Corporation	8	A
ANQ 778	1948	AEC Regent III O961	Commonwealth Engineering H—/—RD	Dept of Road Transport & Tramways, Sydney	984	A
ACC 88	1949	Bedford OB	Duple C29F	Deiniolen Motors		A
CBV 431	1949	Guy Arab III	Crossley H30/26R	Blackburn Corporation	131	A
KTC 615	1949	Guy Arab III	Guy B33R	Accrington Corporation	10	A
KTD 768	1950	Leyland Titan PD2/1	Lydney L27/26R	Leigh Corporation	16	R
FBU 827	1950	Crossley DD42/8	Crossley H30/26R	Oldham Corporation	368	A
BDJ 67	1950	AEC Regent III O961	Park Royal H30/26R	St Helens Corporation	D67	R
EX 6644	1950	Crossley SD42/7	Yeates C35F	W. J. Haylett ('Felix Coaches'), Great Yarmouth		A
GFY 406	1950	Leyland Titan PD2/3	Leyland H30/26R	Southport Corporation	106	A
JND 629	1951	Leyland Titan PD2/3	Metro-Cammell H32/26R	Manchester Corporation	3228	R
BDJ 808	1952	AEC Regent III O961	Park Royal	St Helens Corporation	D8	A
NTF 466	1952	Daimler CVG5	Northern Counties B32F	Lancaster City Transport	466	R
RFM 644	1954	Guy Arab IV	Guy/Park Royal H30/26R	Chester Corporation	4	A
CDJ 878	1954	Leyland Titan PD2/9	Davies H30/26R	St Helens Corporation	E78	A
LDN 96	1955	AEC Regent III 6812A	Roe H33/27RD	York Pullman Bus Co	67	RP
ONE 744+	1956	BUT 9612T	Burlingham H33/26R	Manchester Corporation	1344	R
GDJ 435	1957	AEC Regent V MD3RV	Weymann H33/26R	St Helens Corporation	H135	A
434 BTE	1957	Crossley Regent V D3RV	East Lancs H31/28RD	Darwen Corporation	17	R
KRN 422	1957	Leyland Titan PD2/10	Crossley H33/29R	Preston Corporation	31	R
HDJ 753	1958	AEC Regent V D3RV	Weymann H33/26R	St Helens Corporation	J153	R
453 AUP	1958	AEC Reliance	Plaxton B45F	Wilkinson Bros, Sedgefield	53	R

63

Registration	Date	Chassis	Body	New to	Fleet No	Status
GEN 201	1958	Leyland Titan PD3/6	Weymann H41/32RD	Bury Corporation	201	R
KDJ 999	1959	AEC Regent V 2D3RA	East Lancs H41/32F	St Helens Corporation	K199	A
PFR 346	1959	Leyland Titan PD2/27	Metro-Cammell FH35/28RD	Blackpool Corporation	346	A
FHF 456	1959	Leyland Atlantean PDR1/1	Metro-Cammell H44/33F	Wallasey Corporation	6	A
MSD 407	1959	Leyland Titan PD3/3	Alexander L35/32RD	Western SMT Co	D1543	A
PBN 668	1960	Daimler CVG6/30	East Lancs H41/32F	Bolton Corporation	150	A
LDJ 985	1960	Leyland Titan PD2A/27	Weymann H30/25RD	St Helens Corporation	K175	A
WLT 991	1961	AEC Routemaster R2RH	Park Royal H36/28R	London Transport	RM991	R
562 RTF	1961	Leyland Titan PD2/40	East Lancs H37/28R	Widnes Corporation	31	R
TRJ 109	1962	AEC Reliance 2MU3RV	Weymann B45F	Salford City Transport	109	A
152 CLT	1962	AEC Routemaster R2RH	Park Royal H36/28R	London Transport	RM1152	R
574 TD	1962	Guy Arab IV	Northern Counties H41/32R	Lancashire United Transport	110	R
OWJ 353A	1962	Leyland Titan PD3/4	Roe	Doncaster Corporation	175	R
PSJ 480	1962	Leyland Titan PD2A/27	Massey H37/27F	Wigan Corporation	35	A
TDJ 612	1963	AEC Reliance 2MU3RA	Marshall B45F	St Helens Corporation	212	R
6219 TF	1963	Guy Arab IV	Northern Counties H41/32R	Lancashire United Transport	135	R
201 YTE	1963	Leyland Titan PD2/37	East Lancs O37/28F	Lancaster City Transport	201	R
4227 FM	1964	Bristol Lodekka FS6G	ECW H33/27RD	Crosville Motor Services	DFG157	R
8859 VR	1964	AEC Regent V 2D3RA	East Lancs H41/32R	A. Mayne & Son, Manchester		R
AJA 139B	1964	Bedford VAL14	Strachans B52F	North Western Road Car Co	139	RP
HTF 644B	1964	Leyland Titan PD2/40	East Lancs H37/28R	Widnes Corporation	38	R
HTJ 521B	1964	Guy Arab V	Northern Counties H41/32F	Lancashire United Transport	165	RP
JTD 300B	1964	Guy Arab V	Northern Counties H41/32F	Lancashire United Transport	166	A
FFM 136C	1965	Guy Arab V	Massey H41/32F	Chester Corporation	36	R
CFR 590C	1965	Leyland Titan PD3A/1	Metro-Cammell H41/30R	Blackpool Corporation	390	R
BED 731C	1965	Leyland Titan PD2/40 Special	East Lancs H34/30F	Warrington Corporation	50	R
BCK 367C	1965	Leyland Titan PD3/6	Leyland/PCT H38/32F	Preston Corporation	61	A
WTE 155D	1966	Guy Arab V	Northern Counties H41/30F	Lancashire United Transport	232	R
XTF 98D	1966	Leyland Titan PD3/4	East Lancs H41/32F	Haslingden Corporation	1	A
MDJ 554E	1967	Leyland Titan PD2A/27	East Lancs H37/28R	St Helens Corporation	54	R
MDJ 555E	1967	Leyland Titan PD2A/27	East Lancs H37/28R	St Helens Corporation	55	A
GEX 740F	1968	Leyland Atlantean PDR1/1	Marshall B39F	Great Yarmouth Corporation	40	R
PYM 106F	1968	AEC Reliance 6MU3R	Plaxton C30C	Glenton Tours, London		R
FNC 304F	1968	Bedford VAS5	Duffy/McArdle/Metsec B33F	CIE (Ireland)	SS90	R
LFR 529F	1968	Leyland Titan PD3/11	MCW H41/30R	Blackpool Corporation	529	RP
KJA 299G	1968	Bristol RESL6G	Marshall B43F	North Western Road Car Co	299	R
HCK 204G	1968	Leyland Panther PSUR1A/1R	MCW B47D	Preston Corporation	204	RP
AFM 103G	1969	Bristol RELH6G	ECW C47F	Crosville Motor Services	CRG103	RP
DFM 347H	1969	Guy Arab V	Northern Counties H41/32F	Chester Corporation	47	A
SRJ 328H	1970	Leyland Atlantean PDR2/1	MCW H47/31D	SELNEC PTE	1205	A
JFM 650J	1970	Daimler Fleetline CRG6LX	Northern Counties H43/29F	Chester Corporation	50	A
JDJ 260K	1972	AEC Swift 3MP2R	Marshall B44D	St Helens Corporation	260	R
PDJ 269L	1972	AEC Swift 3MP2R	Marshall B42D	St Helens Corporation	269	RP
JMA 413L	1972	Bristol RELH6L	ECW C49F	North Western Road Car Co	413	R
RTC 645L	1972	Leyland National 1151/1R/0101	Leyland National B52F	Widnes Corporation	1	R
DKC 305L	1972	Leyland Atlantean AN68/1R	Alexander H43/32F	Merseyside PTE	1305	RP
LED 71P	1976	Bristol RESL6G	East Lancs B41D	Warrington Corporation	71	R
LTE 489P	1976	Leyland Leopard PSU3D/2R	Plaxton B48F	Lancashire United Transport	438	R
VBA 151S	1978	Leyland Atlantean AN68A/1R	Northern Counties H43/32F	Greater Manchester PTE	8151	RP
ANA 551Y	1982	Leyland Atlantean AN68D/1R	Northern Counties H43/32F	Greater Manchester PTE	8551	RP

+ Trolleybus

Right: Former Widnes 38 (HTF 644B), an East Lancs-bodied Leyland PD2, new in 1964, is now preserved in its later Halton Livery. *Philip Lamb*

Notes:

KJ 2578	Originally H24/24R; converted to canteen by Liverpool Corporation (CL4)
AFY 971	Originally H26/25R
RV 6360	Originally H26/24R; renumbered 6 following open-top conversion
DKY 713	Rebodied 1960
FFY401 FFY403 FFY404	Originally H30/26R
HLW 159	Acquired by Bradford City Transport (410) in 1958

BDJ 808	Converted to breakdown vehicle by Harper Bros, Heath Hayes
OWJ 353A	Originally registered 475 HDT; converted to breakdown vehicle by South Yorkshire PTE and renumbered M3
PSJ 480	Originally registered JJP 502
201 YTE	Originally H37/28F
BCK 367C	Rebuilt from Leyland PD2 by Preston Corporation
FNC 304F	Originally registered EZL 90 in Irish Republic
DFM 347H	Last Guy Arab delivered to a British operator

Above: Former Maidstone trolleybus 56 (GKP 511), a 1944 Sunbeam rebodied by Roe in 1960, is seen at Sandtoft Trolleybus Centre. *Stephen Morris*

Right: Seen at Sandtoft Trolleybus Centre are (from left to right): former Maidstone 11 (HKR 11), a 1947 Northern Coachbuilders-bodied Sunbeam trolleybus; former Nottingham 137 (OTV 137), a 1953 Park Royal-bodied AEC Regent III motor bus, and former Reading 113 (ARD 676), a 1939 Park Royal-bodied AEC trolleybus. The last is owned by the British Trolleybus Society, whose vehicles appear under a separate heading in Part 2 of this book. *Philip Lamb*

Sandtoft Transport Centre

Contact address: Belton Road, Sandtoft, Doncaster DN8 5SX
Phone: 01724 711391
E-mail: website: www.sandtoft.org.uk
Brief description: Home of the nation's trolleybuses and the Sandtoft Miniature Railway
Events planned: 23/24 April 2000, 30 April/1 May 2000, 28/29 May 2000, 25 June 2000, 9 July 2000, 29/30 July 2000, 13 August 2000, 27/28 August 2000, 24 September 2000, 22 October 2000, 10 December 2000 and 17 December 2000
Opening days/times: 12.00 to 17.00 on the above dates

Directions by car: From M180 junction 2, take A161 southbound to Belton. Turn right and museum is 2 miles on right-hand side.
Directions by public transport: Free bus from Doncaster station at 13.30 on 24 April, 30 July, 28 August and 22 October (please telephone to check operation)
Charges: Adult £3.50, Child/Senior Citizen £2, Family £10
Facilities: A B(e) D E F G H L P R S T
Other information: Coach tours and private party visits can be accommodated at other times by prior arrangement

Registration	Date	Chassis	Body	New to	Fleet No	Status
1425 P+	1932	Fabrique Nationale	B26SD	Liége (Belgium)	425	RP
TV 9333+	1934	Karrier E6	Brush H64R	Nottingham City Transport	367	A
FW 8990+	1937	AEC 661T	Park Royal H30/26R	Cleethorpes Corporation	54	A
FTO 614	1939	AEC Regent O661	-	Nottingham City Transport	802	A
CET 613+	1942	Sunbeam MS2C	East Lancs B39C	Rotherham Corporation	74	A
964 H 87+	1943	Vetra CB60	CTL B17D	Limoges (France)	5	R
GHN 754+	1944	Karrier W	East Lancs H39/31F	Bradford Corporation	792	R
GKP 511+	1944	Sunbeam W	Roe H34/28R	Maidstone Corporation	56	RP
CDT 636+	1945	Karrier W	Roe H34/28R	Doncaster Corporation	375	R
GTV 666+	1945	Karrier W	Brush H30/26R	Nottingham City Transport	468	A
DKY 703+	1945	Karrier W	East Lancs H37/29F	Bradford Corporation	703	R
DKY 706+	1945	Karrier W	East Lancs H37/29F	Bradford Corporation	706	R

Registration	Date	Chassis	Body	New to	Fleet No	Status
RC 8575+	1945	Sunbeam W	Park Royal H30/26R	Derby Corporation	175	A
JV 9901	1947	AEC Regent III O961	Roe H31/25R	Grimsby Corporation	81	RP
HKR 11+	1947	Sunbeam W	Northern Coachbuilders H30/26R	Maidstone Corporation	72	RP
CVH 741+	1947	Sunbeam MS2	Park Royal HR40/30	Huddersfield Corporation	541	RP
KTV 493+	1948	BUT 9611T	Roe H31/25R	Nottingham City Transport	493	R
EKU 743+	1949	BUT 9611T	Roe H33/25R	Bradford Corporation	743	A
EKU 746+	1949	BUT 9611T	Roe H33/25R	Bradford Corporation	746	R
LHN 784+	1949	BUT 9611T	East Lancs H37/29AF	Bradford Corporation	834	R
GDT 421	1949	Daimler CVD6	Roe L27/26R	Doncaster Corporation	112	A
BCK 939	1949	Leyland Titan PD1	-	Preston Corporation	6	R
EKY 558	1949	Leyland Titan PD2/3	Leyland H33/26R	Bradford Corporation	558	RP
GFU 692+	1950	BUT 9611T	Northern Coachbuilders H38/26R	Cleethorpes Corporation	59	RP
KTV 506+	1950	BUT 9641T	Brush H38/32R	Nottingham City Transport	506	R
FET 618+	1950	Daimler CTE6	Roe H40/30R	Rotherham Corporation	44	A
JWW 375+	1950	Sunbeam F4	East Lancs H37/29F	Bradford Corporation	845	A
JWW 376+	1950	Sunbeam F4	East Lancs H37/29F	Bradford Corporation	846	A
JWW 377+	1950	Sunbeam F4	East Lancs H37/29F	Bradford Corporation	847	A
ERD 152+	1950	Sunbeam S7	Park Royal H38/30RD	Reading Corporation	181	A
GAJ 12+	1950	Sunbeam F4	Roe H35/26R	Tees-side Railless Traction Board	2	A
KDT 393	1951	AEC Regent III 9613A	Roe H31/25R	Doncaster Corporation	122	A
BDJ 87+	1951	BUT 9611T	East Lancs H30/26R	St Helens Corporation	387	A
FKU 758+	1951	BUT 9611T	Weymann H33/26R	Bradford Corporation	758	A
OTV 137	1953	AEC Regent III 9613E	Park Royal H30/26R	Nottingham City Transport	137	RP
MDT 222	1953	AEC Regal III 9621A	Roe B39F	Doncaster Corporation	22	R
JDN 668	1954	AEC Regent III 6812A	Roe H33/25RD	York Pullman Bus Co	64	R
TDH 914+	1955	Sunbeam F4A	Willowbrook H36/34RD	Walsall Corporation	864	A
KVH 219+	1956	BUT 9641T	East Lancs H40/32R	Huddersfield Corporation	619	A
XWX 795	1959	AEC Reliance 2MU3RV	Roe C—F	Felix Motors, Doncaster	40	A
9629 WU	1960	AEC Reliance 2MU3RV	Roe DP41F	Felix Motors, Doncaster	41	R
KSK 270+	1960	Schindler SWR Chassisless	Schindler B27T	Schaffhausen (Switzerland)	207	R
VRD 193+	1961	Sunbeam F4A	Burlingham H38/30F	Reading Corporation	193	R
657 BWB	1962	Leyland Atlantean PDR1/1	Park Royal H44/33F	Sheffield Joint Omnibus Committee	1357	R
KHC 369	1963	AEC Regent V 2D3RV	East Lancs H32/28RD	Eastbourne Corporation	69	R
433 MDT	1963	Leyland Tiger Cub PSUC1/11	Roe B45F	Doncaster Corporation	33	R
JTF 920B	1964	AEC Reliance 2MU3RV	Neepsend B—D	Reading Corporation	48	A
KDT 206D	1966	Daimler CVG6LX	Roe H34/28F	Doncaster Corporation	206	RP
66+	1967	Lancia	Dalfa H43/25D	Oporto (Portugal)	140	R
UDT 455F	1968	Leyland Royal Tiger Cub RTC1/2	Roe B45D	Doncaster Corporation	55	R
WWJ 754M	1973	Daimler Fleetline CRG6LXB	Park Royal H43/27D	Sheffield Transport	754	R
ERU 159V	1979	Leyland Fleetline FE30ALR	Alexander H43/31F	Bournemouth Transport	159	R
C45 HDT+	1985	Dennis Dominator DTA1401	Alexander H47/33F	South Yorkshire PTE	2450	R

+ Trolleybus

Notes:

FTO 614	Converted to tower wagon	JWW 375	Rebodied 1962; chassis ex-Mexborough & Swinton
964 H 87	French registration	JWW 376	Rebodied 1963; chassis ex-Mexborough & Swinton
GHN 754	Originally single-decker; rebodied 1958	JWW 377	Rebodied 1963; chassis ex-Mexborough & Swinton
GKP 511	Rebodied 1960	GAJ 12	Rebodied 1964
CDT 636	Rebodied 1955	KSK 270	Registration not carried
DKY 703	Rebodied 1960	657 BWB	Rebodied 1968; renumbered 227 in 1970 following dissolution of JOC
DKY 706	Rebodied 1960		
HKR 11	On loan from Maidstone Borough Council	JTF 920B	Caravan conversion; originally registered 5148 DP
LHN 784	Rebodied 1962; chassis new to Darlington	66	Portuguese registration
BCK 939	Converted to breakdown vehicle	C45 HDT	Experimental vehicle, originally registered B450 CKW
FET 618	Rebodied 1956 (formerly single-decker)		

Above: Pictured in action at Sandtoft is former Nottingham trolleybus 506 (KTV 506), a 1950 Brush-bodied BUT six-wheeler. *Graham Wise*

Below: Another BUT six-wheeled trolleybus is former Huddersfield 619 (KVH 219); new in 1956, it has East Lancs bodywork. *Philip Lamb*

Scottish Vintage Bus Museum   Lathalmond

Contact address: M90 Commerce Park, Lathalmond, Fife, KY12 OSY
Phone: 01383 623380
E-mail: website: www.busweb.co.uk/svbm
Affiliation: NARTM
Brief description: The collection of over 120 buses was, in the main, operated or manufactured in Scotland, from the late 1920s to the early 1980s. Vehicles are generally owned by private individuals or groups. A fully-equipped workshop enables comprehensive restoration to be undertaken. The 42-acre site is a former Royal Navy depot.
Events planned: 19/20 August 2000 — open weekend

Opening days/times: Easter to end of September, Sundays 13.00 to 17.00
Directions by car: Use M90 junction 3. Take B914 Dollar road. Left B915 Dunfermline (2 miles). Half mile to M90 Commerce Park on right.
Directions by public transport: Nearest bus/train Dunfermline. No public transport to site.
Charges: Sunday opening £2. Other charges apply for open weekend.
Facilities: B B(e) D E P R S T

Registration	Date	Chassis	Body	New to	Fleet No	Status
GE 2446	1928	Leyland Titan TD1	Leyland L27/24RO	Glasgow Corporation	111	R
SO 3740	1929	Leyland Tiger TS2	Alexander B32F	Scottish General (Northern) Omnibus Co		R
RU 8678	1929	Leyland Lion PLSC3	Leyland B35F	Hants & Dorset Motor Services	268	A
VD 3433	1934	Leyland Lion LT5A	Alexander B36F	W. Alexander & Sons	P721	R
AAA 756	1935	Albion Victor PK114	Abbott C20C	King Alfred Motor Services, Winchester		R
WG 3260	1935	Leyland Lion LT5A	Alexander B35F	W. Alexander & Sons	P705	A
WG 8107	1939	Leyland Tiger TS8	Alexander	W. Alexander & Sons	P528	R
WG 8790	1939	Leyland Tiger TS8	Alexander B39F	W. Alexander & Sons	P573	A
HF 9126	1940	Leyland Titan TD7	Metro-Cammell	Wallasey Corporation	74	A
ETJ 108	1940	Leyland Tiger TS11	Roe	Leigh Corporation	79	RP
DSG 169	1942	Leyland Titan TD5	Alexander L27/26R	Scottish Motor Traction Co	J66	R
CDR 679	1943	Guy Arab II	Roe	Plymouth Corporation	249	RP
JWS 594	1943	Guy Arab II	Duple/Nudd FH31/24R	Edinburgh Corporation	314	R
BRS 37	1945	Daimler CWD6	Duple H30/26R	Aberdeen Corporation	155	RP
VV 9135	1946	Daimler CWD6	Duple H30/26R	Northampton Corporation	135	A
XG 9304	1947	Leyland Titan PD1A	Northern Counties L27/26R	Middlesbrough Corporation	52	A
AWG 623	1947	AEC Regal I O662	Alexander C30F	W. Alexander & Sons	A36	R
AWG 639	1947	AEC Regal I O662	Alexander C35F	W. Alexander & Sons	A52	R
BWG 39	1948	Bedford OB	SMT C25F	W. Alexander & Sons	W218	RP
BMS 405	1948	Daimler CVD6	Burlingham C33F	W. Alexander & Sons	D10	RP
GGA 670	1948	Foden PVSC6	Plaxton C35F	Scottish Co-operative Whosesale Society, Glasgow		RP
AWG 393	1948	Guy Arab III	Cravens H30/26R	W. Alexander & Sons	RO607	R
ESG 652	1948	Guy Arab III	Metro-Cammell B35R	Edinburgh Corporation	739	R
KTF 589	1949	AEC Regent III 9612E	Park Royal O33/26R	Morecambe & Heysham Corporation	60	R
FSC 182	1949	Daimler CVG6	Metro-Cammell H31/25R	Edinburgh Corporation	135	R
SS 7486	1950	Bedford OB	Duple C29F	Stark's Motor Services, Dunbar	B12	A
SS 7501	1950	Bedford OB	Duple C29F	Fairbairn, Haddington		R
DCS 616	1950	Daimler CVD6	Massey O32/28RD	Hunter (A1), Dreghorn		R
EVA 324	1950	Guy Arab III	Guy B33R	Central SMT Co	K24	R
GVD 47	1950	Guy Arab III	Duple H31/26R	Hutchison's Coaches, Overtown		RP
CWG 283	1950	Leyland Tiger PS1	Alexander C35F	W. Alexander & Sons	PA181	RP
MTE 639	1951	AEC Regent III 6812A	Weymann H33/26R	Morecambe & Heysham Corporation	77	R
DGS 536	1951	Leyland Tiger PS1/1	McLennan C39F	A. & C. McLennan, Spittalfield		R
DGS 625	1951	Leyland Tiger PS1/1	McLennan C39F	A. & C. McLennan, Spittalfield		R
DMS 820	1951	Leyland Tiger OPS2/1	Alexander C35F	W. Alexander & Sons	PB7	A
DMS 823	1951	Leyland Tiger OPS2/1	Alexander C35F	W. Alexander & Sons	PB10	RP
BMS 222	1952	Leyland Royal Tiger PSU1/15	Alexander C41C	W. Alexander & Sons	PC1	RP
CYJ 252	1953	AEC Regent III 9613E	Alexander H32/26R	Dundee Corporation	137	R
NXP 506	1953	Bedford SB	Plaxton C33F	D. Halley, Sauchie		A

Right: HF 9126 is a 1940 Leyland TD7 that was new as Wallasey 74 with conventional double-deck bodywork by Metro-Cammell. In 1952 the bus passed to the Lancashire County Constabulary, which converted it as shown for use as a mobile control post. When this use ceased, the vehicle passed into preservation, and now forms part of the Scottish Vintage Bus Museum's collection. It is seen here with 1940 all-Leyland TD7 JP 4712, formerly Wigan 70 and now with the Manchester Museum of Transport (qv). *Stephen Morris*

Below: A bus more readily associated with Scotland is former Edinburgh 135 (FSC 182), a Daimler CVG6 with Metro-Cammell bodywork, new in 1949. *Philip Lamb*

Registration	Date	Chassis	Body	New to	Fleet No	Status
DWG 917	1953	Leyland Titan PD2/12	Alexander L27/26R	W. Alexander & Sons	RB161	R
LFS 480	1954	Leyland Titan PD2/20	Metro-Cammell H34/29R	Edinburgh Corporation	480	R
GM 6384	1954	Leyland Titan PD2/10	Leyland L27/28R	Central SMT Co	L484	A
TYD 888	1955	AEC Reliance MU3RV	Duple C43F	Wakes Services, Sparkford		R
FWG 846	1955	Bristol LS6G	ECW B45F	W. Alexander & Sons	E11	A
OWS 620	1957	Bristol Lodekka LD6G	ECW H33/27R	Scottish Omnibuses	AA620	RP
OFS 777	1957	Leyland Titan PD2/20	Metro-Cammell H34/29R	Edinburgh Corporation	777	R
OFS 798	1957	Leyland Titan PD2/20	Metro-Cammell H34/29R	Edinburgh Corporation	798	RP
J 1359	1958	Albion Victor FT39KAN	Reading B35F	Jersey Motor Transport Co	5	RP
WUS 248	1959	AEC Reliance 2MU3RA	Plaxton C37F	Cotter's Motor Tours, Glasgow		A
SWS 671	1959	AEC Reliance 2MU3RV	Alexander C38F	Scottish Omnibuses	B671	R
SWS 715	1959	AEC Reliance 2MU3RV	Park Royal C41F	Scottish Omnibuses	B715	A
1252 EV	1959	Bristol MW5G	ECW DP41F	Eastern National Omnibus Co	488	R
YYS 174	1960	Bedford C5Z1	Duple C21FM	David MacBrayne, Glasgow	54	R
XSL 945A	1960	Bristol MW6G	Alexander C41F	Western SMT Co	T1590	A
XSN 25A	1960	Bristol MW6G	Alexander C41F	Western SMT Co	T1591	A
RAG 578	1960	Daimler CVG6LX-30	Northern Counties FH41/32F	J. Hunter (A1), Kilmarnock		A
WLT 371	1960	AEC Routemaster R2RH	Park Royal H36/28R	London Transport	RM371	RP
EDS 50A	1960	AEC Routemaster R2RH	Park Royal H36/28R	London Transport	RM560	R
EDS 320A	1961	AEC Routemaster R2RH	Park Royal H36/28R	London Transport	RM606	A
EDS 288A	1961	AEC Routemaster R2RH	Park Royal H36/28R	London Transport	RM910	R
RAG 411	1961	Bristol Lodekka LD6G	ECW H33/27RD	Western SMT Co	B1645	R
RCS 382	1961	Leyland Titan PD3A/3	Alexander L35/32RD	Western SMT Co	D1684	R
UCX 275	1961	Guy Wulfrunian	Roe H43/32F	County Motors, Lepton	99	R
VSC 86	1961	Leyland Tiger Cub PSUC1/3	Weymann B47F	Edinburgh Corporation	86	R
YSG 101	1961	Leyland Leopard PSU3/2R	Alexander B33T	Edinburgh Corporation	101	R
YYJ 914	1961	Leyland Tiger Cub PSUC1/2	Alexander C41F	Stark's Motor Services, Dunbar	H8	A
7424 SP	1962	AEC Reliance 2MU3RV	Alexander C41F	W. Alexander & Sons (Fife)	FAC4	R
LDS 201A	1963	AEC Routemaster 2R2RH	Park Royal H36/28R	London Transport	RM1607	R
UCS 659	1963	Albion Lowlander LR3	Northern Counties H40/31F	Western SMT Co	N1795	R
AFS 91B	1964	AEC Reliance 4MU3RA	Alexander B53F	Scottish Omnibuses ('Eastern Scottish')	B91	R
ARG 17B	1964	AEC Reliance 2MU3RA	Alexander C41F	W. Alexander & Sons (Northern)	NAC246	A
ASC 665B	1964	Leyland Titan PD3/6	Alexander H41/29F	Edinburgh Corporation	665	R
AWA 124B	1964	Bedford SB13	Duple C41F	J. O. Andrew, Sheffield		R
BXA 452B	1964	Bristol Lodekka FS6G	ECW H33/27RD	W. Alexander & Sons (Fife)	FRD187	A
BXA 464B	1964	Bristol Lodekka FS6G	ECW H33/27RD	W. Alexander & Sons (Fife)	FRD199	RP
CUV 203C	1965	AEC Routemaster R2RH	Park Royal H36/28R	London Transport	RM2203	R
ESF 801C	1965	Leyland Atlantean PDR1/1	Alexander H43/31F	Edinburgh Corporation	801	R
FFV 447D	1966	AEC Reliance 2U3RA	Plaxton C45F	J. Abbott & Sons, Blackpool		RP
KBD 714D	1966	Bristol Lodekka FS6G	ECW H33/27RD	United Counties Omnibus Co	714	A
EWS 168D	1966	Bristol RELH6G	Alexander C38Ft	Scottish Omnibuses ('Eastern Scottish')	XA168	A
NMY 634E	1967	AEC Routemaster R2RH/2	Park Royal H32/24F	British European Airways	8241	R
LUS 524E	1967	AEC Reliance 2U3RA	Willowbrook C49F	David MacBrayne, Glasgow	150	R
HFV 757E	1967	AEC Reliance 6MU3R	Plaxton C41F	J. Abbott & Sons, Blackpool		A
GRS 343E	1967	Albion Viking VK43AL	Alexander DP40F	W. Alexander & Sons (Northern)	NNV43	R
HDV 639E	1967	Bristol MW6G	ECW C39F	Western National Omnibus Co	1434	R
KPM 91E	1967	Bristol Lodekka FLF6G	ECW O32/28F	Brighton, Hove & District Omnibus Co	91	R
HGM 335E	1967	Bristol Lodekka FLF6G	ECW H44/34F	Central SMT Co	BL335	R
HGM 346E	1967	Bristol Lodekka FLF6G	ECW H44/34F	Central SMT Co	BL346	R
JSC 900E	1967	Leyland Atlantean PDR2/1	Alexander O47/35F	Edinburgh Corporation	900	R
NTY 416F	1968	AEC Reliance 6MU3R	Plaxton C45F	J. Rowell, Prudhoe		RP
KGM 664F	1968	Leyland Leopard PSU3/1R	Alexander B53F	Central SMT Co	T64	A
VMP 8G	1968	Albion Viking VK43AL	Alexander DP40F	Road Transport Industry Training Board	16	A
VMP 10G	1969	AEC Reliance 6U3ZR	Alexander B57F	Road Transport Industry Training Board	24	R

Registration	Date	Chassis	Body	New to	Fleet No	Status
NAG 120G	1969	Bristol REMH6G	Alexander C42Ft	Western SMT Co	T2214	RP
XFM 42G	1969	Guy Arab V	Northern Counties H41/32F	Chester Corporation	42	R
TMS 585H	1970	Leyland Leopard PSU3/1R	Alexander C49F	Road Transport Industry Training Board	84	RP
VFU 864J	1971	Bedford J2	Plaxton C—F	Hardings, Lincolnshire		A
TGM 214J	1971	Daimler Fleetline CRG6LX	ECW H43/34F	Central SMT Co	D14	RP
AMS 513K	1972	Leyland Leopard PSU3/3R	Alexander	W. Alexander & Sons (Midland)	MPE113	R
BWG 833L	1972	Leyland Leopard PSU3/3R	Alexander B53F	W. Alexander & Sons (Midland)	MPE133	A
BFS 1L	1972	Leyland Atlantean AN68/1R	Alexander H45/30D	Edinburgh Corporation	1	R
BFS 463L	1972	Bedford YRQ	Alexander DP45F	Scottish Omnibuses ('Eastern Scottish')	C463	A
YSD 350L	1973	Leyland Leopard PSU3/3R	Alexander B41F	Western SMT Co	L2390	R

Above: In the years 1954-7 Edinburgh Corporation received no fewer than 300 Metro-Cammell-bodied Leyland PD2s. These initially caused doubts as to their durability, owing to their lightweight construction, but they confounded their critics and many put in 20 years' service. Three are now preserved at Lathalmond, including 777 (OFS 777), one of the final batch. *Stephen Morris*

Registration	Date	Chassis	Body	New to	Fleet No	Status
BWS 105L	1973	Seddon Pennine IV-236	Seddon DP25F	Edinburgh Corporation	105	RP
RJI 5722	1974	Leyland Leopard PSU3B/4R	Plaxton C53F	Barton Transport, Chilwell	1428	RP
SCS 333M	1974	Leyland Leopard PSU3/3R	Alexander B53F	Western SMT Co	L2464	RP
KSF 1N	1975	Ailsa B55-10	Alexander H44/35F	W. Alexander & Sons (Fife)	FRA1	R
NCS 16P	1976	Leyland Fleetline FE30AGR	Alexander H43/31F	Hill (A1), Stevenston		RP
MSF 750P	1976	Seddon Pennine VII	Alexander C42Ft	Scottish Omnibuses ('Eastern Scottish')	XS750	R
SSC 212P	1976	Ailsa B55-10	Alexander H—/—F	Tayside Regional Council	107	RP
SMS 120P	1976	Daimler Fleetline CRG6LXB	Alexander H44/31F	W. Alexander & Sons (Midland)	MRF120	RP
RRS 46R	1977	Leyland Leopard PSU3E/4R	Duple C49F	W. Alexander & Sons (Northern)	NPE46	R
OSJ 629R	1977	Leyland Leopard PSU3C/3R	Alexander B53F	Western SMT Co	L2629	RP
XMS 252R	1977	Leyland Leopard PSU3C/3R	Alexander B53F	W. Alexander & Sons (Midland)	MPE252	A
NDL 656R	1977	Bristol VRTSL3/6LXB	ECW H43/31F	Southern Vectis Omnibus Co	656	RP
CSG 773S	1978	Ailsa B55-10	Alexander H44/35F	Scottish Omnibuses ('Eastern Scottish')	VV773	A
CSG 792S	1978	Seddon Pennine VII	Plaxton C45F	Scottish Omnibuses ('Eastern Scottish')	S792	RP
LSC 936T	1978	Seddon Pennine VII	Alexander DP49F	Scottish Omnibuses ('Eastern Scottish')	S936	A
JSX 595T	1979	Leyland Atlantean AN68A/1R	Alexander H45/30D	Lothian Region Transport	595	A
LIL 9929	1979	Bedford PJK	Plaxton C29F	Blood Transfusion Service		RP
SSX 602V	1979	Seddon Pennine VII	Alexander B53F	Scottish Omnibuses ('Eastern Scottish')	S602	RP
DSD 936V	1979	Seddon Pennine VII	Alexander C49F	Western SMT Co	S2936	A
CH 9399	1980	Guy Victory Mk 2	Alexander H60/24D	China Motor Bus	LV36	R
RHS 400W	1980	Wales & Edwards	Wales & Edwards B12F	South of Scotland Electricity		R
FES 831W	1981	Volvo B58-61	Duple B59F	Stagecoach, Perth		A
HSC 173X	1981	Leyland Cub CU435	Duple B31F	Lothian Region Transport	173	RP

Notes:

SO 3740 — Passed to W. Alexander & Sons in 1930; numbered P63 in 1932 and rebodied in 1934

VD 3433 — Rebodied 1945

WG 8107 — Breakdown vehicle

HF 9126 — Originally H28/26R; acquired by Lancashire County Constabulary in 1952 and converted for use as mobile control post

ETJ 108 — Breakdown vehicle

DSG 169 — Alexander body to Leyland design; converted to open-top in 1959 and restored in 1980/1

CDR 679 — Converted to platform lorry for farm use in 1963

JWS 594 — Originally London Transport G77 (GLL 577); rebuilt and rebodied 1953

KTF 589 — Originally H33/26R

SS 7486 — Passed to Scottish Omnibuses (C22) in 1964

DCS 616 — Rebodied in 1958 as H32/28RD

GVD 47 — Acquired by McGill's Bus Services, Barrhead, in 1952

XSL 945A — Originally registered OCS 712

XSN 25A — Originally registered OCS 713

WLT 371 — Acquired by Kelvin Scottish Omnibuses (1910) in 1986

EDS 50A — Originally registered WLT 560; acquired by Stagecoach, Perth, in 1985

EDS 320A — Originally registered WLT 606; acquired by Kelvin Scottish Omnibuses (1919) in 1986

EDS 288A — Originally registered WLT 910; acquired by Kelvin Scottish Omnibuses (1929) in 1986

UCX 275 — On loan from Dewsbury Bus Museum

YYJ 914 — Originally registered ESS 989

LDS 201A — Originally registered 607 DYE; acquired by Stagecoach, Perth, in 1986

NMY 634E — Passed to London Transport (RMA50) in 1979; acquired by Stagecoach, Perth, in 1987

HDV 639E — First vehicle operated by Stagecoach

KPM 91E — Originally H38/32F; acquired by Scottish Omnibuses (AA971) in 1973 and converted to open-top (as OT2) in 1983

JSC 900E — Originally H47/35F

AMS 513K — Originally C49F; converted to breakdown vehicle

YSD 350L — Originally C49F; rebuilt and shortened by Western SMT in 1980

RJI 5722 — Originally registered PAL 796M

SSC 212P — Display vehicle; originally registered LES 44P

NDL 656R — Acquired by Lowland Scottish Omnibuses (856) in 1991

LIL 9929 — Original identity unknown

CH 9399 — Hong Kong registration

RHS 400W — Battery-electric bus

FES 831W — First new vehicle delivered to Stagecoach (as C50Ft)

Sheffield Bus Museum

Tinsley

Contact address: Tinsley Tram Sheds, Sheffield Road, Tinsley, Sheffield S9 2FY
Phone: 0114 255 3010
E-mail: website:
http://freespace.virgin.net/neil.worthington/sheff/page1~1.htm
Brief description: The display of over 20 vehicles is housed in part of a former tram shed.
Events planned:
23 April 2000, 11 June 2000, 13 August 2000 — open days;
10 September 2000 — Meadowhall Rally;
8 October 2000, 10 December 2000 — open days.

Opening days/times: Open days as above; also most Saturdays and Sundays (not Christmas) 12.00 to 16.00 (please telephone to check opening times before travelling).
Directions by car: From M1 Junction 34 take A6178
Directions by public transport: By Supertram to Carbrook (200yd from museum); also good bus links from Sheffield and Rotherham.
Charges: Adult £1, concession 50p, Family £2.
Facilities: B(e)

Registration	Date	Chassis	Body	New to	Fleet No	Status
WG 9180	1940	Leyland Titan TD7	Leyland L27/26R	W. Alexander & Sons	P266	R
GWJ 724	1941	AEC Regent O661		Sheffield Corporation	G54	A
JWB 416	1947	Leyland Tiger PS1	Weymann B34R	Sheffield Corporation	216	A
KWE 255	1948	AEC Regent III 9612E		Sheffield Corporation	G55	A
HD 7905	1948	Leyland Tiger PS1	Brush B34F	Yorkshire Woollen District Transport Co	622	RP
ACW 645	1950	Leyland Titan PD2/1	Leyland H30/26R	Burnley, Colne & Nelson Joint Committee	63	R
MHY 765	1950	Leyland Comet ECPO/1R	Duple C32F	Orient Coaches, Bristol		RP
OWE 116	1952	AEC Regent III 9613A	Roe H33/25R	Sheffield Joint Omnibus Committee	116	A
KET 220	1954	Daimler CVG6	Weymann H30/26R	Rotherham Corporation	220	RP
RWB 87	1954	Leyland Titan PD2/12	Weymann H32/26R	Sheffield Corporation	687	RP
WRA 12	1955	AEC Monocoach MC3RV	Park Royal B45F	Booth & Fisher, Halfway		R
VDV 760	1958	Bristol Lodekka LD6G	ECW H33/27RD	Western National Omnibus Co	1943	A
PFN 858	1959	AEC Regent V 2LD3RA	Park Royal FH40/32F	East Kent Road Car Co		A
TDK 322	1959	AEC Regent V D2RA	Weymann H33/28RD	Rochdale Corporation	322	R
TET 135	1959	Daimler CVG6-30	Roe	Rotherham Corporation	135	A
6330 WJ	1960	AEC Regent V 2D3RA	Roe H39/30RD	Sheffield Joint Omnibus Committee	1330	A
7874 WJ	1960	AEC Regent V 2D3RA	Alexander H37/32R	Sheffield Corporation	874	R
1322 WA	1961	AEC Reliance 2MU3RA	Plaxton C36F	Sheffield United Tours	322	A
NAT 766A	1962	Daimler CVG6-30	Roe H39/31F	Grimsby & Cleethorpes Joint Transport Committee	57	RP
GHD 765	1962	Leyland Titan PD3A/1	Metro-Cammell H39/31F	Yorkshire Woollen District Transport Co	893	R
BWB 148H	1969	Leyland Atlantean PDR2/1	Park Royal H—/—D	Sheffield Joint Omnibus Committee	1148	A
DWB 54H	1970	AEC Swift 5P2R	Park Royal B50F	Sheffield Transport	54	RP
AHA 451J	1971	Leyland Leopard PSU4B/4R	Plaxton C40F	BMMO ('Midland Red')	6451	R
UWA 296L	1973	Leyland Atlantean AN68/1R	Alexander H43/31F	Sheffield Transport	296	RP
MGE 183P	1975	Ailsa B55-10	Alexander H44/35F	Greater Glasgow PTE	AV8	A
LWB 383P	1976	Ailsa B55-10	Van Hool-McArdle H44/31D	South Yorkshire PTE	383	R
LWB 388P	1976	Ailsa B55-10	Van Hool-McArdle H44/31D	South Yorkshire PTE	388	RP
PSJ 825R	1977	Ailsa B55-10	Van Hool-McArdle H44/31F	J. Hunter (A1), Kilmarnock		R

Notes:

GWJ 724	Originally bus 462; converted to grit wagon	NAT 766A	Originally registered TJV 100
KWE 255	Originally bus 255; converted to grit wagon	BWB 148H	Renumbered 748 in 1970 following dissolution of JOC
TET 135	Originally H39/31F; converted to breakdown vehicle	PSJ 825R	Originally H44/31D

Top: The Sheffield Bus Museum is home to these two AEC Regents, which were converted to gritting wagons following withdrawal from normal service. GWJ 724 had been new as 462 in 1941, and KWE 255 as 255 in 1948. *Philip Lamb*

Left: A more modern vehicle at Sheffield is UWA 296L, an Alexander-bodied Leyland Atlantean new to the city's Transport Department in 1973 as 296. *Philip Lamb*

Right: Former Salford 511 (FRJ 511) is a Daimler CVG6/Metro-Cammell delivered in 1951. Now part of the Tameside Transport Collection, it is seen at the 1999 Ribble Club rally in Blackpool. Note that 'Salford City Transport' takes the place of the usual 'Daimler' on the fluted radiator-top. *Paul Wigan*

Tameside Transport Collection   Mossley

Contact address: Roaches Industrial Estate, Manchester Road, Mossley, Greater Manchester

Brief description: A working museum comprising a small but varied collection of vehicles ranging from 1929 to the1960s. There is in addition a display of transport-related items.

Opening days/times: Last weekend of each month, 10.00 to 15.00; visits at other times by prior appointment.

Directions by car:
From Ashton-under-Lyne take A635 (Huddersfield) through Mossley. Museum is 1 mile on right-hand side, adjacent to Shadows Lane.

Directions by public transport:
Bus service 355 from Ashton-under-Lyne or Oldham. By rail to Mossley station (approximately 1 mile walk).

Charges: No charge but donations welcome.

Facilities: D S R T

Other information: Car parking is limited.

Registration	Date	Chassis	Body	New to	Fleet No	Status
LG 2637	1929	Crossley Arrow	Crossley B32R	S. Jackson & Sons, Crewe		A
DNF 204	1937	Crossley Mancunian	Metro-Cammell/Crossley B32R	Manchester Corporation	129	RP
HG 9651	1948	Leyland Tiger PS1/1	Brush B35R	Burnley, Colne & Nelson Joint Committee	10	R
DBN 978	1949	Crossley SD42/7	Crossley B32R	Bolton Corporation	8	R
JND 728	1950	Daimler CVG6	Metro-Cammell H32/26R	Manchester Corporation	4127	R
FRJ 511	1951	Daimler CVG6	Metro-Cammell H30/24R	Salford City Transport	511	R
CRC 911	1952	Crossley DD42/8A	Brush H30/26R	Derby Corporation	111	R
422 CAX	1961	AEC Regent V MD3RV	Massey L31/28R	Bedwas & Machen UDC	5	R
7209 PW	1962	Bedford J2SZ2	Plaxton C20F	H. & I. Jarvis, Downham Market		R
105 UTU	1962	Leyland Titan PD2/37	Northern Counties H36/28F	SHMD Board	5	RP
BWO 585B	1964	AEC Regent V 2MD3RV	Massey L31/28R	Bedwas & Machen UDC	8	R
NMA 328D	1966	Daimler Fleetline CRG6LX	Northern Counties H43/31F	SHMD Board	28	RP

Notes:
LG 2637   Passed to Crosville Motor Services (U2) in 1934

Contact address: Howth Castle Demesne, Howth, Dublin 13, Ireland
Phone: (00) 353 1 832 0427
Affiliation: NARTM
Brief description: The museum is run by a group of volunteers dedicated to the preservation and restoration of valuable road transport heritage. Exhibits include buses, trams and commercial, public utility, military, fire-appliance, electric and horse-drawn vehicles. Other displays include transport-associated memorabilia. The museum is a registered charity.
Opening days/times:
June to August: Monday to Saturday 10.00 to 17.00; Sunday 14.00 to 17.00.

September to May: Saturdays, Sundays and Bank Holidays 14.00 to 17.00.
Directions by car: Howth is 9 miles north of Dublin City Centre or 7 miles from the M1/M50 junction at Dublin Airport. Museum is located in grounds of Howth Castle Demesne.
Directions by public transport: Bus 31 from Dublin City Centre; to Howth Castle then 10min walk. Local DART rail service to Howth station, then half mile walk.
Charges: Adult £1.60, Child 80p, Family £4 (group discounts available).
Facilities: E G P T
Other information: Limited access for disabled.

Registration	Date	Chassis	Body	New to	Fleet No	Status
TE 5110	1928	Leyland Lion PLSC3	(chassis only)	Colne Corporation	22	A
*	1933	AEC Regal I	(chassis only)	(unknown)		A
ZI 9708	1933	Dennis Lancet I	DUTC B32R	Dublin United Tramways Co	F21	A
ZC 714	1937	Leyland Titan TD4	Leyland H32/26R	Dublin United Tramways Co	R1	R
FRU 305	1945	Bristol K6A	Hants & Dorset FO31/28R	Hants & Dorset Motor Services	1108	A
GZ 7628	1947	Leyland Tiger PS1	NIRTB B34R	Northern Ireland Road Transport Board	A8560	A
ZD 7163	1948	Leyland Tiger OPS3	(chassis only)	CIE	P23	A
ZH 3926	1948	AEC Regal III O962	Park Royal C35R	Great Northern Railway (Ireland)	427	A
ZH 3937	1948	AEC Regent III 9612E	Park Royal H30/26RD	Great Northern Railway (Ireland)	438	R
ZH 4538	1948	Leyland Titan PD2/3	Leyland H33/27R	CIE	R389	R
IY 1940	1949	AEC Regent III 9621E	Park Royal O33/26R	Morcambe & Heysham Corporation	58	A
LTU 869	1949	Commer Avenger I	Plaxton C33F	Thornley, Woodley		A
ZL 2718	1950	GNR-Gardner	Park Royal/GNR B—R	Great Northern Railway (Ireland)	387	A
MZ 7396	1950	Guy Arab III	Harkness B31F	Belfast Corporation	298	A
GUX 188	1951	Bedford OB	Duple B31F	Lloyd, Oswestry		A
IY 7384	1951	GNR-Gardner	Park Royal/GNR DP33R	Great Northern Railway (Ireland)	390	RP
ZJ 5933	1951	Leyland Tiger OPS3	CIE	CIE	P193	A
OZ 6686	1953	Daimler CVG6	Harkness H30/26R	Belfast Corporation	432	A
ZL 6816	1953	Leyland Titan OPD2/1	CIE H37/31R	CIE	R506	A
ZO 6819	1953	Leyland Tiger PS2/14	CIE B39R	CIE	P309	A
ZO 6857	1953	Leyland Tiger PS2/14	CIE B39R	CIE	P347	R
ZY 79	1954	AEC Regal IV 9822E	Park Royal/GNR B45R	Great Northern Railway (Ireland)	274	A
ZO 6949	1954	Leyland Royal Tiger PSU1/15	CIE B39D	CIE	U78	A
ZO 6881	1954	Leyland Royal Tiger PSU1/15	CIE C34C	CIE	U10	A
ZU 9241	1955	Leyland Titan OPD2/1	CIE H37/31RD	CIE	R567	A
CYI 621	1958	Leyland Titan OPD2/2	CIE	CIE	R819	A
UI 8511	1960	Leyland Tiger Cub PSUC1/5	Dundalk B45F	Londonderry & Lough Swilly Railway Co	83	A
HZA 230	1960	Leyland Titan PD3/2	CIE H41/33R	CIE	RA105	RP
HZA 279	1961	AEC Regent V 2D2RA	CIE H41/28RD	CIE	AA2	A
404 RIU	1963	Albion Lowlander LR1	Alexander H41/31F	W. Alexander & Sons (Midland)	MRE38	A
NZE 598	1964	Leyland Leopard L2	CIE B45F	CIE	E170	A
NZE 620	1964	Leyland Titan PD3A/6	Park Royal H41/33R	CIE	R911	A
NZE 629	1965	Leyland Titan PD3A/6	Park Royal O—/—R	CIE	R920	A
EZH 17	1965	Leyland Leopard PSU3/4R	CIE B45F	CIE	C17	A
EZH 64	1965	Leyland Leopard PSU3/4R	CIE/NEHB	CIE	C64	A
EZH 231	1966	Leyland Leopard PSU3/4R	CIE B53F	CIE	C231	A
VZL 179	1966	Bedford VAL14	Plaxton C53F	Wallace Arnold Tours, Leeds		A
WZJ 724	1967	Bedford VAM14	Duffy C45F	P. O'Grady, Santry		A
EZL 1	1967	Bedford VAS5	CIE B33F	CIE	SS1	RP

Registration	Date	Chassis	Body	New to	Fleet No	Status
VZI 44	1967	Leyland Atlantean PDR1/1	CIE H43/35F	CIE	D44	A
*	1971	Bedford VAL70	Duffy B40D	Aer Lingus	301	A
694 ZO	1975	Leyland Atlantean AN68/1R	Van Hool-McArdle H45/29D	CIE	D694	A
ZJ 5933				Breakdown vehicle		

Notes:

*	Not registered
FRU 305	Originally numbered TD774; renumbered in 1950 and rebodied 1952
IY 1940	Originally H38/26R, registered KTF 587
ZL 2718	Ambulance conversion
CYI 621	Breakdown vehicle
404 RIU	Originally registered VWG 376
NZE 629	Originally H41/33R
EZH 64	Originally B45F; converted to mobile hospital
VZL 179	Originally registered EUG 907D

Above: Preserved by the Transport Museum Society of Ireland is former NIRTB (Northern Ireland Road Transport Board) A8560 (GZ 7628) a Leyland PS1 bodied by the operator and new in 1947. *Stephen Morris*

Right: Also at the TMSI is former CIE (Coras Iompair Eireann) R389 (ZH 4538) a 1948 all-Leyland PD2. *Stephen Morris*

Ulster Folk & Transport Museum Cultra

Contact address: Cultra, Holywood, Co Down, BT18 OEU
Phone: 028 9042 8428
Affiliation: National Museums and Galleries of Northern Ireland
Brief description: A unique collection of wheeled vehicles from cycles to trams, buses and cars. Interpretive exhibitions show the development of road transport. Not all the vehicles listed are always on display. Please enquire before your visit if you wish to see a particular vehicle.

Opening days/times: All the year round but closing for a few days at Christmas time. From 09.30 or 10.30 on weekdays and 12.00 on Sundays (please 'phone for details)
Directions by car: On A2 Belfast-Bangor road
Directions by public transport: On main Belfast-Bangor railway and bus routes
Charges: £4 (discounts for groups)
Facilities: A D E F G L P R T

Registration	Date	Chassis	Body	New to	Fleet No	Status
CZ 7013	1935	Dennis Lancet I	Harkness B31F	Belfast Corporation	102	R
IL 2849	1937	Leyland Cheetah LZ1	(chassis only)	Erne Bus Co, enniskillen		A
ZD 726	1941	GNR-Gardner	GNR B35F	Great Northern Railway (Ireland)	324	RP
GZ 783	1942	Bedford OWB	Ulsterbus B32F	Northern Ireland Road Transport Board	V957	R
GZ 1882	1944	Daimler CWA6	Harkness H30/26R	Belfast Corporation	214	A
GZ 4696	1946	Leyland Tiger PS1	(chassis only)	Northern Ireland Road Transport Board	Z800	A
FZ 7883+	1948	AEC 664T	Harkness/Park Royal H36/32R	Belfast Corporation	98	A
FZ 7897+	1948	Guy BTX	Harkness H36/32R	Belfast Corporation	112	R
EOI 4857	1973	Daimler Fleetline CRG6LX-33	Alexander (Belfast) H49/37F	Belfast Corporation	857	R
KIJ 4035	1978	Dodge S56	Wright B25F	North Eastern Education & Library Board		A

+ Trolleybus

Notes:

ZD 726	Rebodied 1949	EOI 4857	Passed to Citybus (2857) in 1973; rebodied 1976
GZ 783	Body rebuilt 1985		

Above: The oldest bus in the care of the Ulster Folk & Transport Museum is former Belfast 102 (CZ 7013), a 1935 Dennis Lancet with Harkness bodywork. *Stephen Morris*

Wirral Transport Museum   Birkenhead

Contact address: Pacific Road, Birkenhead, Merseyside, L41 5HN
Phone: 0151 666 2756
Brief description: The museum houses a collection of buses, tram-cars, motor cycles, cars and a few military vehicles. Some of the trams and buses are being restored by local enthusiast groups. Trams operate during weekends and some school holidays.
Events planned: n/a

Opening days/times: Please telephone for details
Directions by car: Adjacent to Woodside ferry terminal
Directions by public transport: Bus or ferry to Woodside
Other information: At the time of writing, the museum is closed for repairs, but is expected to open in April/May 2000 — please phone for details.

Registration	Date	Chassis	Body	New to	Fleet No	Status
BG 8557	1944	Guy Arab II	Massey H31/26R	Birkenhead Corporation	242	R
BG 9225	1946	Leyland Titan PD1	Massey H30/26R	Birkenhead Corporation	106	RP
AHF 850	1951	Leyland Titan PD2/1	Metro-Cammell H30/26R	Wallasey Corporation	54	R
GM 5875	1953	Leyland Titan PD2/10	Leyland	Central SMT Co	L475	
RFM 641	1953	Guy Arab IV	Massey H30/26R	Chester Corporation	1	R
CHF 565	1956	Leyland Titan PD2/10	Burlingham H30/26R	Wallasey Corporation	106	RP
FBG 910	1958	Leyland Titan PD2/40	Massey H31/28R	Birkenhead Corporation	10	R
FHF 451	1958	Leyland Atlantean PDR1/1	Metro-Cammell H44/33F	Wallasey Corporation	1	R
KFF 367	1962	AEC Routemaster R2RH	Park Royal H36/28R	London Transport	RM1101	R
RCM 493	1964	Leyland Leopard L1	Massey B42D	Birkenhead Corporation	93	R
GCM 152E	1967	Leyland Titan PD2/37	Massey H36/30R	Birkenhead Corporation	152	RP
UFM 52F	1968	Bristol RELL6G	ECW DP50F	Crosville Motor Services	ERG52	R
OFM 657K	1972	Daimler Fleetline CRG6LX	Northern Counties 43/29F	Chester Corporation	57	R
THM 692M	1974	Daimler Fleetline CRL6	MCW H44/24D	London Transport	DMS1692	R
CWU 146T	1979	Leyland Fleetline FE30AGR	Roe H43/33F	West Yorkshire PTE	7146	R

Notes:

BG 8557	Rebodied 1953
GM 5857	Originally L27/26R; acquired by W. Alexander & Sons (Midland) and converted to breakdown vehicle (ML245)
CHF 565	Carries 1949 body

KFF 367	Originally registered 101 CLT
OFM 957K	Originally H43/29F; rebodied 1984 and converted to open-top (renumbered 57) in 1998
THM 692M	Promotional vehicle for Museum
CWU 146T	Promotional vehicle for The Hamilton Quarter

Below: Pictured at their Birkenhead home are three vehicles from the Wirral Transport Museum. UFM 52F is a dual-purpose ECW-bodied Bristol RELL, new as Crosville ERG52 in 1968 and restored to its later NBC livery; Leyland Atlantean/Metro-Cammell FHF 451 has the first production Atlantean chassis and is generally believed to have been the first of its type to enter service, as Wallasey No 1 in 1958; that same year, by contrast, Birkenhead took delivery of 10 (FBG 910), a Massey-bodied Leyland PD2. *Philip Lamb*

Former Blackpool 554 (PFR 554H) is a Marshall-bodied AEC Swift dating from 1970, now owned by the Lancastrian Transport Trust. *Philip Lamb*

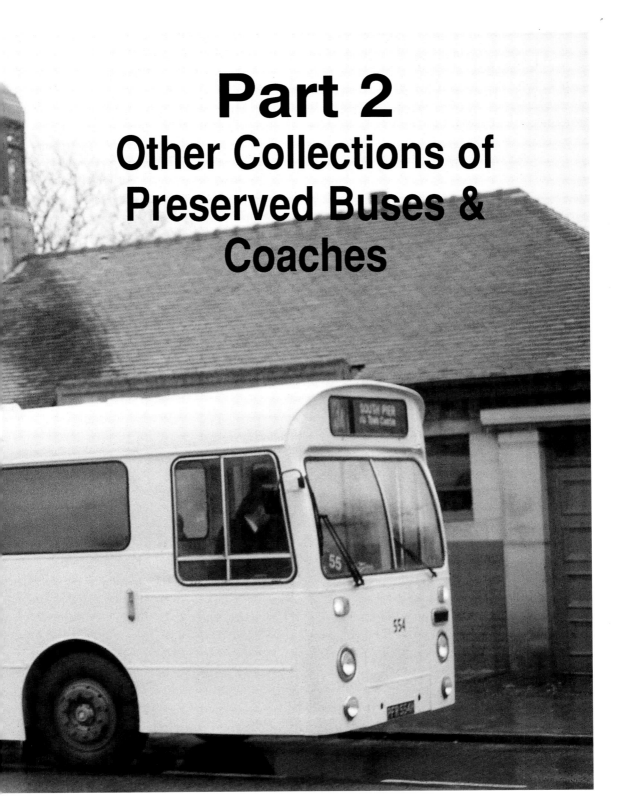

Part 2
Other Collections of Preserved Buses & Coaches

Aldershot & District Bus Interest Group

Contact address: 111 Park Barn Drive, Guildford, Surrey, GU2 6ER
E-mail: website: sites.netscape.net/ashleyhoare/homepage
Affiliation: NARTM, FBHVC.
Brief description: The group was formed in 1994 to consolidate the collection of ex-Aldershot & District preserved vehicles and other artefacts which had been saved over the years. The vehicles range from 1920s Dennis E types to Dennis, AEC and Bristol buses which entered service in the 1960s and 1970s at the very end of the company's existence. The vehicles in the collection are in the care of members of an associated group which also welcomes the owners of other preserved Dennis buses and coaches.
Events planned: Running days on 30 April/1 May 2000 based at Aldershot and Farnborough.
Opening days/times: Running days are held from time to time at which many of the operational vehicles may be seen in service.
Other information: Regular working parties; new members welcome.

Registration	Date	Chassis	Body	New to	Fleet No	Status
RD 111	1928	Dennis G	(unknown) T17	Reading Fire Brigade		R
OT 8283	1928	Dennis E	(chassis only)	Aldershot & District Traction Co	D210	A
OT 8592	1928	Dennis E	Strachan & Brown	Aldershot & District Traction Co	D217	A
OT 8898	1928	Dennis E	Strachan & Brown	Aldershot & District Traction Co	D226	A
OU 1805	1929	Dennis E	(chassis only)	Aldershot & District Traction Co	D283	A
TE 7870	1929	Dennis ES	Brush B29D	Accrington Corporation	57	R
CC 8670	1929	Dennis GL	Roberts T19	Llandudno UDC		R
CC 8671	1929	Dennis GL	Roberts T19	Llandudno UDC		R
CC 9424	1930	Dennis GL	Roberts T20	Llandudno UDC		A
MJ 4549	1932	Dennis Lancet I	Short B32F	Smith, Westoning		R
TJ 836	1933	Dennis Dart	Duple C20F	Entwhistle, Morecambe		R
JG 8720	1937	Dennis Lancet II	Park Royal B35R	East Kent Road Car Co		RP
GAA 580	1948	Dennis Lancet J3	Strachans B32R	Aldershot & District Traction Co	944	RP
GAA 616	1948	Dennis Lancet J3	Strachans C32R	Aldershot & District Traction Co	980	RP
GOU 845	1950	Dennis Lance K3	East Lancs L25/26R	Aldershot & District Traction Co	145	R
HOU 904	1950	Dennis Lancet J10	Strachans B38R	Aldershot & District Traction Co	178	R
LAA 231	1953	Dennis Lancet J10C	Strachans FC38R	Aldershot & District Traction Co	196	RP
MOR 581	1954	AEC Reliance MU3RV	MCW B40F	Aldershot & District Traction Co	543	R
LOU 48	1954	Dennis Lance K4	East Lancs L28/28R	Aldershot & District Traction Co	220	R
POR 428	1956	Dennis Falcon P5	Strachans B30F	Aldershot & District Traction Co	282	RP
SOU 456	1958	Dennis Loline I	East Lancs H37/31RD	Aldershot & District Traction Co	348	RP
SOU 465	1958	Dennis Loline I	East Lancs H37/31RD	Aldershot & District Traction Co	357	R
XHO 370	1960	AEC Reliance 2MU3RV	Weymann DP40F	Aldershot & District Traction Co	370	R
462 EOT	1962	Dennis Loline III	Alexander H39/29F	Aldershot & District Traction Co	462	A
488 KOT	1964	Dennis Loline III	Weymann H39/29F	Aldershot & District Traction Co	488	RP
AAA 503C	1965	Dennis Loline III	Weymann H39/29F	Aldershot & District Traction Co	503	R
AAA 506C	1965	Dennis Loline III	Weymann H39/29F	Aldershot & District Traction Co	506	R
AAA 508C	1965	Dennis Loline III	Weymann H39/29F	Aldershot & District Traction Co	508	A
CCG 296K	1971	Bristol RESL6G	ECW B40D	Aldershot & District Traction Co	651	RP

Notes:

RD 111	Replica body	JG 8720	Rebodied 1949
OT 8283	Originally Dennis F, converted to E type	MOR 581	Rebodied 1967
TE 7870	Body rebuilt 1974 by Wyatt		

Above right: Members of the associated group own some Dennis vehicles from other operators, including this former Llandudno 1929 Dennis GL with Roberts toastrack body. *Philip Lamb*

Right: Members of the group own no fewer than nine former Aldershot & District Dennis double-deckers, three of which are seen here at Guildford station. 220 (LOU 48) is a 1954 Lance with lowbridge East Lancs body, while 357 (SOU 465) and 348 (SOU 456) are from the 1958 batch of Dennis Lolines, also with East Lancs bodywork but to centre-gangway layout, thanks to the chassis design. *Paul Wigan*

Aycliffe & District Bus Preservation Society

Contact address: 110 Fewston Close, Newton Aycliffe, Co Durham, DL5 7HF
Affiliation: NARTM; North East Museums Ltd
Brief description: A collection of Darlington area service buses, fully restored and in running order.
Events planned: -
Opening days/times: Viewing by prior appointment only.

Registration	Date	Chassis	Body	New to	Fleet No	Status
GHN 189	1942	Bristol K5G	ECW L27/26R	United Automobile Services	BGL29	R
LHN 860	1948	Bristol L5G	ECW B35F	United Automobile Services	BG413	R
304 GHN	1958	Bristol LS6B	ECW C39F	United Automobile Services	BUC4	RP
AHN 451B	1964	Daimler CCG5	Roe H32/31R	Darlington Corporation	7	R
NDL 769G	1969	Bristol LHS6L	Marshall B35F	Southern Vectis Omnibus Co	833	R

Notes:

GHN 189	1948 body fitted in 1954
304 GHN	Now fitted with Gardner engine
NDL 769G	Acquired by United Automobile Services (1452) in 1977

Bolton Bus Group

Contact address: 12 Arundale, Westhoughton, Bolton BL5 3YB
Brief description: A small group of enthusiasts formed to preserve examples of Bolton's buses. The vehicles are displayed at Bury Transport Museum, which can be visited by prior arrangement.
Opening days/times: Please write to the above address to arrange a visit

Registration	Date	Chassis	Body	New to	Fleet No	Status
NBN 436	1959	Leyland Titan PD3/4	East Lancs H41/32F	Bolton Corporation	128	RP
SBN 767	1961	AEC Regent V 2D3RA	Metro-Cammell H40/32F	Bolton Corporation	167	RP
FBN 232C	1965	Leyland Atlantean PDR1/1	East Lancs H45/33F	Bolton Corporation	232	R
TWH 809K	1971	Leyland Atlantean PDR2/1	East Lancs H49/37F	SELNEC PTE	6809	R

Above: The Aycliffe & District Bus Preservation Society owns a small collection of vehicles which operated in northeast England. Marshall-bodied Bristol LHS NDL 769G was actually new to Southern Vectis in 1969, but passed to United in 1977. In 1981 it received this special livery for working the 'Newtonian' service in Newton Aycliffe. It is seen here in Brighton on the occasion of the 1999 HCVS Rally. *Paul Cripps*

Right: The Bolton Bus Group's collection includes long-wheelbase Leyland Atlantean/East Lancs TWH 809K. Ordered by Bolton Corporation, it was delivered new to Bolton's successor, SELNEC, in 1971. *Philip Lamb*

Bournemouth Heritage Transport Collection

Phone: 01202 636007
Brief description: The collection comprises vehicles, mainly from Bournemouth Corporation or the Bournemouth area, built between the years 1928 and 1979. Most are owned by the Bournemouth Passenger Transport Association Ltd, which is a registered charity.

Events planned: Please see the enthusiast press for details
Opening days/times: Owing to storage relocation, the collection is not currently open to the public. It is hoped to arrange an event during 2000. Please see the enthusiast press for details

Registration	Date	Chassis	Body	New to	Fleet No	Status
LJ 500	1928	Karrier WL6/1	Hall Lewis B40D	Bournemouth Corporation	33	RP
VH 6188	1934	AEC Regent I O661	Hall Lewis H—/—R	Huddersfield Corporation	119	A
VH 6217	1934	AEC Regent I 661	Lee Motors	Huddersfield Corporation	120	R
BOW 162	1938	Bristol L6B	-	Hants & Dorset Motor Services	TS669	RP
DKY 711+	1944	Karrier W	East Lancs H37/29F	Bradford Corporation	711	A
DKY 712+	1944	Karrier W	East Lancs H37/29F	Bradford Corporation	712	A
HLJ 44	1948	Bristol K6A	ECW L27/28R	Hants & Dorset Motor Services	TD895	A
NNU 234+	1949	BUT 9611T	Weymann H32/26R	Nottinghamshire & Derbyshire Traction Co	353	RP
JLJ 403	1949	Leyland Tiger PS2/3	Burlingham FDP35F	Bournemouth Corporation	46	R
KEL 110	1949	Leyland Titan PD2/3	Weymann FH33/25D	Bournemouth Corporation	110	R
KEL 133	1950	Leyland Titan PD2/3	Weymann FH27/21D	Bournemouth Corporation	247	R
KLJ 346+	1950	BUT 9641T	Weymann H31/25D	Bournemouth Corporation	212	R
NLJ 268	1953	Leyland Royal Tiger PSU1/13	Burlingham B—F	Bournemouth Corporation	258	A
NLJ 272	1953	Leyland Royal Tiger PSU1/13	Burlingham B42F	Bournemouth Corporation	262	R
RRU 901	1955	Leyland Tiger Cub PSUC1/1	Park Royal B42F	Bournemouth Corporation	264	R
RRU 904	1955	Leyland Tiger Cub PSUC1/1	Park Royal B42F	Bournemouth Corporation	267	R
YLJ 147	1959	Leyland Titan PD3/1	Weymann H37/25D	Bournemouth Corporation	147	R
8154 EL	1960	Leyland Titan PD3/1	Weymann H37/25D	Bournemouth Corporation	154	R
NMR 345	1960	Leyland Titan PD3/1	Weymann H37/25D	Bournemouth Corporation	155	RP
8156 EL	1960	Leyland Titan PD3/1	Weymann O37/25D	Bournemouth Corporation	156	R
297 LJ+	1962	Sunbeam MF2B	Weymann H37/28D	Bournemouth Corporation	297	R
6167 RU	1963	Leyland Titan PD3A/1	Weymann H39/30F	Bournemouth Corporation	167	R
ALJ 340B	1964	Daimler Fleetline CRG6LX	MH Cars H44/33F	Bournemouth Corporation	40	R
AEL 170B	1964	Leyland Atlantean PDR1/1	Weymann H43/31F	Bournemouth Corporation	170	R
CRU 103C	1965	Leyland Leopard PSU3/2R	Weymann DP45F	Bournemouth Corporation	103	R
CRU 180C	1965	Daimler Fleetline CRG6LX	Weymann CO43/31F	Bournemouth Corporation	180	R
ERV 247D	1966	Leyland Atlantean PDR1/1	MCW O43/33F	Portsmouth Corporation	247	RP
FJY 915E	1967	Leyland Atlantean PDR1/1	MCW O43/32F	Plymouth Corporation	215	RP
KRU 55F	1967	Daimler Roadliner SRC6	Willowbrook B49F	Bournemouth Corporation	55	A
ORU 230G	1969	Leyland Atlantean PDR1A/1	Alexander H43/31F	Bournemouth Corporation	230	R
VRU 124J	1971	Daimler Fleetline CRG6LXB	Roe H43/31F	Hants & Dorset Motor Services	1901	R
XRU 277K	1972	Leyland Atlantean PDR1A/1	Alexander H43/31F	Bournemouth Corporation	277	RP
DLJ 111L	1973	Daimler Fleetline CRL6	Alexander O43/31F	Bournemouth Corporation	111	R
DLJ 116L	1973	Daimler Fleetline CRL6	Alexander H43/31F	Bournemouth Corporation	116	R
DLJ 119L	1973	Daimler Fleetline CRL6	Alexander H43/31F	Bournemouth Corporation	119	A
FEL 105L	1973	Leyland Leopard PSU3B/4R	Plaxton C47F	Bournemouth Corporation	105	A
ERU 156V	1979	Leyland Fleetline FE30ALR	Alexander H43/31F	Bournemouth Transport	156	A

+ Trolleybus

Notes:

VH 6188	Chassis new 1934, fitted with 1930 body	NMR 345	Originally reg 8155 EL
VH 6217	Converted to tower wagon in 1948	8156 EL	Originally H37/25D
BOW 162	New with Beadle body; converted to breakdown vehicle	ERV 247D	Originally H43/33F
DKY 711	Rebodied 1960	FJY 915E	Originally H43/32F
DKY 712	Rebodied 1960	DLJ 111L	Originally H43/31F
NLJ 268	Originally B42F; used as canteen at Chesterfield 1970-81		

Above: Former Bournemouth 156 (8156 EL) is a Weymann-bodied Leyland PD3 of 1960 which has been converted to open-top for sightseeing tours of its home town. This view shows the dual-door layout — unusual on front-engined buses but a feature of Bournemouth's deliveries for many years. *Philip Lamb*

Below: RRU 904 is a Park Royal-bodied Leyland Tiger Cub, new as Bournemouth 267 in 1955. This too was originally a dual-door vehicle. *Philip Lamb*

Bristol Aero Collection

Contact address: 37 Corbett Road, Hollywood, Birmingham
B47 5LP
Affiliation: NARTM
Brief description: A collection of Bristol buses housed in an aircraft hangar alongside a display of Bristol aircraft and other products from the companies originally founded by Sir George White.

Events planned: Please see the enthusiast press for details.
Opening days/times: The site is only open by prior arrangement and for special events; there is no public access except for pre-arranged visits.

Registration	Date	Chassis	Body	New to	Fleet No	Status
HW 6634	1929	Bristol B	(chassis only)	Bristol Tramways & Carriage Co		A
JHT 802	1946	Bristol K6A	ECW H30/26R	Bristol Tramways & Carriage Co	C3386	RP
LHW 918	1949	Bristol L5G	ECW B35R	Bristol Tramways & Carriage Co	2410	A
MHU 49	1949	Bedford OB	Duple B30F	Bristol Tramways & Carriage Co	207	RP
JEL 257	1949	Bristol K5G	ECW L27/28R	Hants & Dorset Motor Services	1238	A
LFM 753	1950	Bristol L6B	ECW DP31R	Crosville Motor Services	KW172	R
NFM 67	1952	Bristol KSW6B	ECW H32/28R	Crosville Motor Services	MW435	A
OHY 938	1952	Bristol KSW6B	ECW L27/28RD	Bristol Tramways & Carriage Co	L8089	RP
RTT 996	1954	Bristol Lodekka LD6B	ECW H33/27RD	Southern National Omnibus Co	1876	A
UHY 359	1955	Bristol KSW6B	ECW H32/28R	Bristol Tramways & Carriage Co	C8319	A
UHY 384	1955	Bristol KSW6G	ECW H32/28RD	Bristol Tramways & Carriage Co	8336	RP
YHT 958	1958	Bristol Lodekka LD6B	ECW O33/25RD	Bristol Omnibus Co	L8462	RP
980 DAE	1959	Bristol MW5G	ECW B45F	Bristol Omnibus Co	2960	A
969 EHW	1959	Bristol Lodekka LD6G	ECW H33/25RD	Bath Electric Tramways	L8515	R
972 EHW	1959	Bristol Lodekka LD6B	ECW H33/28R	Bristol Omnibus Co	LC8518	RP
904 OFM	1960	Bristol SC4LK	ECW C33F	Crosville Motor Services	CSG655	RP
Q507 VHR	1961	Bristol MW6G	ECW	Bristol Omnibus Co	W151	A
7682 LJ	1962	Bristol Lodekka FL6G	ECW H70RD	Hants & Dorset Motor Services	1482	A
507 OHU	1962	Bristol Lodekka FLF6B	ECW H38/32F	Bristol Omnibus Co	7062	RP
862 RAE	1962	Bristol SUS4A	ECW B30F	Bristol Omnibus Co	301	R
RDB 872	1964	Dennis Loline III	Alexander H39/32F	North Western Road Car Co	872	A
BHU 92C	1965	Bristol MW6G	ECW DP43F	Bristol Omnibus Co	2428	R
CWN 629C	1965	Bristol MW6G	ECW B45F	United Welsh Services	134	A
FHT 15D	1966	Bristol Lodekka FLF6G	ECW H—/—F	Bristol Omnibus Co	7240	A
FHU 59D	1966	Bristol Lodekka FLF6B	ECW H38/32F	Bristol Omnibus Co	C7246	A
DFE 172D	1966	Bristol Lodekka FLF6G	ECW H38/32F	Lincolnshire Road Car Co	2716	A
DFE 963D	1966	Bristol Lodekka FS5G	ECW H33/27RD	Lincolnshire Road Car Co	2537	R
RDV 423H	1970	Bristol RELH6G	ECW C45F	Western National Omnibus Co (Royal Blue)	1472	R
LRN 60J	1970	Bristol VRLLH6L	ECW CH42/18Ct	W. C. Standerwick	60	R
GYC 160K	1971	Bristol LH6L	ECW B45F	Hutchings & Cornelius Services, South Petherton		RP
HAX 399N	1975	Bristol LHS6L	Duple C35F	R. I. Davies & Son, Tredegar		RP
KHU 326P	1976	Bristol LH6L	ECW B43F	Bristol Omnibus Co	376	RP
TWS 910T	1979	Bristol VRTSL3/6LXB	ECW H43/27D	Bristol Omnibus Co	5129	R

Notes:
YHT 958   Originally H33/25RD
Q507 VHR   Originally coach 2111, registered 404 LHT; converted to
           breakdown vehicle in 1974
507 OHU   On display at Aston Manor Road Transport Museum
FHT 15D   Ex-playbus; to become exhibition vehicle

Above: One of the best-known vehicles in the Bristol Aero Collection is BHU 92C, a 1965 Bristol MW/ECW coach. Formerly Bristol Omnibus 2428, it is restored to its original Bristol Greyhound livery used by the company for its express services, and was photographed arriving in Southsea for the 1997 'Spectacular'.
Philip Lamb

Right: The collection also includes a number of vehicles which have yet to be restored. Amongst these is former Bristol Omnibus 7240 (FHT 15D), a 1966 Bristol FLF/ECW, which is to become an exhibition vehicle.
Philip Lamb

British Trolleybus Society

Contact address: 8 Riding Lane, Hildenborough, Tonbridge, Kent, TN11 9HX

Brief description: The British Trolleybus Society is a contributor society to the Sandtoft Transport Centre. Vehicles from the collection of trolleybuses can be seen from time to time at Sandtoft on display.

Events planned: Details given in the section on Sandtoft Transport Centre

Registration	Date	Chassis	Body	New to	Fleet No	Status
WW 4688	1927	Garrett O type	Garrett B32C	Mexborough & Swinton Traction Co	34	A
RD 7127	1935	AEC Regent II O661	Park Royal L26/26R	Reading Corporation	47	R
ALJ 973	1935	Sunbeam MS2	Park Royal H31/25D	Bournemouth Corporation	99	RP
CU 3593	1937	Karrier E4	Weymann H29/26R	South Shields Corporation	204	A
ARD 676	1939	AEC 661T	Park Royal H30/26R	Reading Corporation	113	R
CKG 193	1942	AEC 664T	Northern Counties H38/32R	Cardiff Corporation	203	A
HYM 812	1948	BUT 9641T	Metro-Cammell H40/21D	London Transport	1812	RP
NDH 959	1951	Sunbeam F4	Brush H34/31R	Walsall Corporation	342	RP
XDH 72	1956	Sunbeam F4A	Willowbrook H36/34RD	Walsall Corporation	872	R
AC-L 379	1956	Henschel 562E	Ludewig RB17/44T	Aachen (Germany)	22	R
FYS 839	1958	BUT 9613T	Crossley H37/34R	Glasgow Corporation	TB78	RP
PVH 931	1959	Sunbeam S7A	East Lancs H40/32R	Huddersfield Corporation	631	R

All the above are trolleybuses, apart from RD 7127. All vehicles are kept at Sandtoft Transport Centre, apart from XDH 72 (see Notes)

Notes:

NDH 959	Rebuilt/lengthened in 1965
XDH 872	Last Walsall trolleybus; on display at Aston Manor Road Transport Museum
AC-L 379	German registration

Cardiff & South Wales Trolleybus Project

Contact address: 211 Hillrise, Llanedeyrn, Cardiff CF23 6UQ

Affiliation: NARTM

Website: http://members.xoom.com/trolleybus

Brief description: The only trolleybus preservation group in the principality of Wales. A regular newsletter is issued, and new members are always welcome.

Registration	Date	Chassis	Body	New to	Fleet No	Status
DKY 704	1945	Karrier W	East Lancs H37/29F	Bradford Corporation	704	RP
EBO 919	1949	BUT 9641T	Bruce H38/29D	Cardiff Corporation	262	RP
KBO 961	1955	BUT 9641T	East Lancs B40R	Cardiff Corporation	243	A
DHW 293K	1972	Bristol LH6L	ECW B42F	Bristol Omnibus Co	353	

All vehicles are trolleybuses except DHW 293K

Notes:

DKY 704	Rebodied in 1959
EBO 919	Body built on East Lancs frames
DHW 293K	Support vehicle

Chelveston Preservation Society

Contact address: 36 Moor Road, Rushden, Northants, NN10 9SP
Brief description: The group has its origins with a small number of employees of United Counties. The collection has evolved to represent most types of Bristol chassis from a range of former Tilling group companies.

Registration	Date	Chassis	Body	New to	Fleet No	Status
VV 5696	1937	Bristol JO5G	ECW B35R	United Counties Omnibus Co	450	R
MPU 21	1948	Bristol K6B	ECW L27/28R	Eastern National Omnibus Co	3960	RP
HPW 108	1949	Bristol K5G	ECW H30/26R	Eastern Counties Omnibus Co	LKH108	A
NAE 3	1950	Bristol L6B	ECW FC31F	Bristol Tramways & Carriage Co	2467	RP
CNH 860	1952	Bristol LWL6B	ECW B39R	United Counties Omnibus Co	860	R
CNH 862	1952	Bristol LWL6B	ECW DP33R	United Counties Omnibus Co	428	R
HWV 294	1952	Bristol KSW5G	ECW L27/28R	Wilts & Dorset Motor Services	365	A
RFM 408	1954	Bristol Lodekka LD6B	ECW H33/25R	Crosville Motor Services	ML663	A
KNV 337	1954	Bristol KSW6B	ECW L27/28R	United Counties Omnibus Co	964	R
TUO 497	1956	Bristol LS6G	ECW B45F	Southern National Omnibus Co	1781	RP
VVF 543	1957	Bristol SC4LK	ECW B35F	Eastern Counties Omnibus Co	LC543	RP
RFU 689	1958	Bristol SC4LK	ECW DP33F	Lincolnshire Road Car Co	2611	R
OPN 807	1959	Bristol Lodekka LDS6B	ECW H33/27R	Brighton, Hove & District Omnibus Co	7	A
827 BWY	1963	Bristol MW6G	ECW B45F	West Yorkshire Road Car Co	SMG19	RP
GAX 2C	1965	Bristol RELL6G	ECW B54F	Red & White Services	R2.65	RP
EDV 555D	1966	Bristol SUL4A	ECW B36F	Southern National Omnibus Co	692	RP
OWC 182D	1966	Bristol MW6G	ECW C34F	Tilling's Transport	T312	R
MMW 354G	1969	Bristol RELL6G	ECW B45D	Wilts & Dorset Motor Services	824	R
HAH 537L	1972	Bristol LH6P	ECW B45F	Eastern Counties Omnibus Co	LH537	RP
MCA 620P	1975	Bristol LH6L	ECW B43F	Crosville Motor Services	SLL620	R

Notes:

VV 5696	Rebodied 1949
CNH 860	Renumbered 426 in 1952; Gardner 5LW engined fitted 1956
CNH 862	Gardner 5LW engine fitted 1956

RFM 408	Eighth production Lodekka; currently has no engine or gearbox
OWC 182D	Passed to Eastern National (392) in 1968 and to Tilling's Travel (9392) in 1971

Right: The Chelveston Preservation Society's collection consists entirely of Bristol/ECW vehicles. The oldest of these is former United Counties 450 (VV 5696), a 1937 JO-type rebodied in 1949. The bus is seen in Chelveston in July 1998. *John Robinson*

Chesterfield 123 Group

Contact address: 87 Broom Drive, Grassmoor, Chesterfield, Derbyshire, S42 5AH
Brief description: The group owns the small collection of Chesterfield vehicles listed, which are shown at rallies throughout the season.

Registration	Date	Chassis	Body	New to	Fleet No	Status
NNU 123M	1973	Daimler Fleetline CRL6	Roe H42/29D	Chesterfield Corporation	123	R
NNU 124M	1973	Daimler Fleetline CRL6	Roe H42/29D	Chesterfield Corporation	124	R

Dewsbury Bus Museum

Contact address: 5 Oakenshaw Street, Agbrigg, Wakefield WF1 5BT
Brief description: The group was formed in the early 1970s and concentrated on ex-West Riding vehicles. By 1989 the collection had grown and, to provide covered accommodation, a new, 14-vehicle shed was erected. Vehicles can be seen at local events, or on site by appointment.

Events planned: 1 May 2000: Rally at Crow Nest Park, Dewsbury
Opening days/times: Open only on rally days and when work is being done on vehicles (please enquire before visiting)
Other information: Other events are being planned — please see enthusiast press for details.

Registration	Date	Chassis	Body	New to	Fleet No	Status
TY 9608	1932	AEC Regal 662	Strachans C28R	Orange Bros, Bedlington	42	A
DHN 475	1939	Bristol L5G	ECW B35R	United Automobile Services	BLO 11	A
AHL 694	1947	Leyland Tiger PS1/1	Barnaby B35F	J. Bullock & Sons, Featherstone	284	RP
BHL 682	1948	Leyland Titan PD2/1	Leyland L27/26R	West Riding Automobile Co	640	RP
TWY 8	1950	Albion CX39N	Roe L27/26RD	South Yorkshire Motors	81	RP
NHU 2	1951	Bristol LSX5G	ECW B44F	Bristol Tramways & Carriage Co	2800	RP
EHL 336	1952	Leyland Tiger PS2/13A	Roe C35F	West Riding Automobile Co	725	A
EHL 344	1952	Leyland Tiger PS2/12A	Roe B39F	West Riding Automobile Co	733	R
JHL 708	1956	AEC Reliance MU3RV	Roe B44F	West Riding Automobile Co	808	RP
JHL 983	1957	AEC Reliance MU3RV	Roe C41C	West Riding Automobile Co	803	R
KHL 855	1957	Guy Arab IV	Roe L29/26RD	West Riding Automobile Co	855	RP
TWT 123	1958	Bristol MW5G	ECW DP41F	West Yorkshire Road Car Co	EUG 71	RP
924 AHY	1958	Bristol MW5G	ECW B45F	Bristol Omnibus Co	2934	A
5228 NW	1959	Leyland Titan PD3/5	Roe H38/32R	Leeds City Transport	228	A
LEN 101	1960	Guy Wulfrunian	(chassis only)	Bury Corporation	101	A
574 CNW	1962	Daimler CVG6	Roe H39/31F	Leeds City Transport	574	RP
PJX 35	1962	Leyland Leopard L1	Weymann B42F	Halifax Corporation	35	A
WHL 970	1963	Guy Wulfrunian	Roe H43/32F	West Riding Automobile Co	970	A
CUV 208C	1965	AEC Routemaster R2RH	Park Royal H38/28R	London Transport	RM2208	R
LHL 164F	1967	Leyland Panther PSUR1/1	Roe B51F	West Riding Automobile Co	164	R
THL 261H	1970	Bristol RELL6G	ECW B53F	West Riding Automobile Co	261	RP
MCK 229J	1971	Leyland Panther PSUR1B/1R	Pennine B47D	Preston Corporation	229	RP
TDL 567K	1972	Bristol RELL6G	ECW B53F	Southern Vectis Omnibus Co	867	A
WEX 685M	1973	AEC Swift 3MP2R	ECW B43D	Great Yarmouth Corporation	85	RP
MUA 865P	1976	Leyland Atlantean AN68/1R	Roe H43/30F	Yorkshire Woollen District Transport Co	768	R

Notes:
TWY 8   New in 1950, registered JWT 112; rebodied and re-registered in 1958
NHU 2   Prototype Bristol LS
MUA 865P   Rebodied 1981

Above: Prior to selling out to the Transport Holding Co in 1967, West Riding was the country's largest independent operator. A number of its vehicles are now preserved at Dewsbury Bus Museum, including 733 (EHL 344), a Roe-bodied Leyland Tiger of 1952, seen in Huddersfield in 1998. *David Reed*

East Pennine Transport Group

Contact address: 23 George Street, Lindley, Huddersfield HD3 3LY
Affiliation: Transport Trust; Keighley Bus Museum
Brief description: An active group progressing with the restoration of a number of interesting vehicles. Please write to the Huddersfield address if you wish to arrange a visit.

Events planned: 13 August 2000 — Kirklees Historic Vehicle Parade
Opening days/times: Visits to workshop only; strictly by prior arrangement.

Registration	Date	Chassis	Body	New to	Fleet No	Status
BRM 596	1936	Leyland Titan TD4	ECW L27/28R	Cumberland Motor Services	291	RP
AVH 470+	1938	Karrier E6	Park Royal H36/28R	Huddersfield Corporation	470	A
CCX 777	1945	Daimler CWA6	Duple L27/28R	Huddersfield Joint Omnibus Committee	217	RP
CCX 801	1945	Guy Arab II	Roe L27/26R	County Motors, Lepton	70	RP
FVH 1	1951	Guy Arab UF	Park Royal B43F	Huddersfield Joint Omnibus Committee	1	RP
HVH 234	1954	AEC Regent III 9613E	East Lancs L30/28R	Huddersfield Joint Omnibus Committee	234	RP
8340 U	1958	Leyland Tiger Cub PSUC1/2	Burlingham C41F	Wallace Arnold Tours, Leeds		RP
CBA 966L	1973	Bedford J2SZ2	Plaxton C15F	Salford Social Services		R
+ Trolleybus						

Notes:
BRM 596   Rebodied 1950
CCX 801   Rebodied 1955

Left: Former Cumberland 291 (BRM 596) has a 1936 TD4 chassis which was rebodied by ECW in 1950. The bus is now preserved by the East Pennine Transport Group, and was photographed in Keighley in March 1996. *John Robinson*

Friends of King Alfred Buses

Contact address: 27 White Dirt Lane, Catherington, Waterlooville, Hampshire, PO8 ONB
E-mail: FOKABevents@lineone.net
Website: http://website.lineone.net/~fokab
Brief description: The collection includes 12 former King Alfred

Motor Services vehicles that have been rescued from around the world and restored. A charitable trust, FoKAB aims eventually to establish a museum. In the meantime, the vehicles can be viewed at the annual running day and other events.
Events planned: 1 Jan 2001 — Annual running day at Winchester.

Registration	Date	Chassis	Body	New to	Fleet No	Status
OU 9286	1931	Dennis 30cwt	Short B18F	King Alfred Motor Services		R
HOR 493	1949	Leyland Titan PD2/1	Leyland H30/26R	Isle of Man Road Services	72	A
JAA 708	1950	Leyland Olympic HR40	MCW B40F	King Alfred Motor Services		RP
POU 494	1956	Leyland Titan PD2/24	East Lancs L27/28R	King Alfred Motor Services		R
WCG 104	1959	Leyland Tiger Cub PSUC1/1	Weymann B45F	King Alfred Motor Services		R
326 CAA	1961	Bedford SB3	Harrington C41F	King Alfred Motor Services		R
595 LCG	1964	AEC Renown 3B2RA	Park Royal H43/31F	King Alfred Motor Services		R
596 LCG	1964	AEC Renown 3B2RA	Park Royal H43/31F	King Alfred Motor Services		R
CCG 704C	1965	Bedford VAL14	Plaxton C49F	King Alfred Motor Services		RP
HOR 590E	1967	Leyland Atlantean PDR1/2	Roe O43/31F	King Alfred Motor Services		R
HOR 592E	1967	Leyland Atlantean PDR1/2	Roe H43/33F	King Alfred Motor Services		R
UOU 417H	1970	Leyland Panther PSUR1A/1R	Plaxton B52F	King Alfred Motor Services		R
UOU 419H	1970	Leyland Panther PSUR1A/1R	Plaxton B52F	King Alfred Motor Services		R
YDW 756K	1972	Scania BR111MH	MCW B40D	Newport Corporation	56	R

Notes:

HOR 493	To be restored as King Alfred vehicle; originally registered KMN 502
POU 494	Repatriated from the USA in 1993
595 LCG	On loan from the Oxford Bus Museum
596 LCG	Repatriated from the USA in 1988

HOR 590E	Originally H43/33F; acquired by Bristol Omnibus Co (8602) and converted to open-top in 1979
HOR 592E	Acquired by Bristol Omnibus Co (8600) and converted to open-top in 1979; restored using roof from sister vehicle HOR 591E

Right: 'King Alfred Motor Services' was the trading name of R. Chisnell & Sons, the Winchester independent taken over by Hants & Dorset in 1973. Leyland Atlantean/Roe HOR 592E was the company's last double-deck delivery, in 1967. Following a number of years spent working as an open-topper in Weston-super-Mare, it was restored by the Friends of King Alfred Buses, and is pictured 'back home' in the Broadway, Winchester. *Philip Lamb*

Golcar Transport Collection

Contact address: 45 Cowlersley Lane, Cowlersley, Huddersfield HD4 5TZ
Affiliation: HCVS
Brief description: A unique collection of Karrier vehicles, most of which are long-term restoration projects. The collection includes two WL6 six-wheeled saloons.

Opening days/times: Collection opens to coincide with craft weekends at the Colne Valley Museum; can be opened at other times by prior arrangement.

Registration	Date	Chassis	Body	New to	Fleet No	Status
*	1922	Karrier	(unknown) B20F	(unknown)		A
WT 9156	1925	Karrier JH	Strachan & Brown B26F	Premier Transport, Keighley		RP
DY 5029	1928	Karrier JKL	London Lorries C26D	A. Timpson & Sons, Catford	117	A
TE 5780	1928	Karrier WL6	English Electric B32F	Ashton-under-Lyne Corporation	8	RP
KD 3185	1928	Karrier WL6	Liverpool Corporation B38R	Liverpool Corporation		A
VH 2088	1929	Karrier ZA	(unknown) B14F	(unknown)		RP
RB 4757	1932	Commer Centaur	Reeve & Kenning B14D	A. G. Fox, Alfreton		RP
JC 5313	1938	Guy Wolf	Waveney C20F	Llandudno UDC		R
14 PKR	1961	Karrier BFD	Plaxton C14F	W. Davis & Sons, Sevenoaks		RP

Notes:

*	unregistered solid-tyred, disc-wheeled chassis	VH 2088	Period body acquired from Anglesey
WT 9156	Body originally on EH 4960	RB 4757	Carries 1929 body from Ford AA chassis

Left: An unusual type favoured by Llandudno was the Guy Wolf; JC 5313 is a 1938 Waveney-bodied example. Now part of the Golcar Transport Collection, it is seen ascending the Great Orme during the 1998 Llandudno Transport Festival. *Philip Lamb*

Right: Bristol L-type LHT 911 was new to Bristol Tramways in 1948; 10 years later it received a 1950 body, which had also been built by Bristol. Nowadays the senior vehicle in the Kelvin Amos Collection, it was photographed (appropriately) at the 1998 Bristol Festival of Transport. *David Reed*

Huddersfield Passenger Transport Group

Contact address: 20 Alma Drive, Dalton, Huddersfield HD5 9EF
Brief description: The collection is based in Huddersfield and comprises nearly 20 vehicles, including commercial vehicles and trams. There are currently six buses in the collection.

Opening days/times: Please contact the above address for an appointment to view.

Registration	Date	Chassis	Body	New to	Fleet No	Status
ECX 425	1949	AEC Regent III 9612E	Northern Coachbuilders L29/26R	Huddersfield Joint Omnibus Committee	225	RP
EFV 300	1951	Leyland Titan PD2/5	Burlingham FH29/23C	Blackpool Corporation	300	RP
ODE 182	1952	Sentinel STC6	Sentinel B44F	Edwards Bros, Crymych		RP
WBR 246	1963	Atkinson Alpha PM746HL	Marshall B43D	Sunderland Corporation	46	RP
HVH 472D	1966	Daimler CVG6LX-30	East Lancs H41/29F	Huddersfield Corporation	472	R
JWU 244N	1975	Leyland Leopard PSU4C/4R	Plaxton B43F	West Yorkshire PTE	8501	RP

Notes:
JWU 244N   Originally DP43F

Kelvin Amos Collection

Contact address: 30 Blandford Close, Nailsea, Bristol BS48 2QQ
Brief description: The two vehicles in the collection are regularly shown and run on free bus services.
Events planned: 17 May 2000 — Transport display at Bristol harbourside.

Registration	Date	Chassis	Body	New to	Fleet No	Status
LHT 911	1948	Bristol L5G	BBW B35R	Bristol Tramways & Carriage Co	2388	R
KED 546F	1968	Leyland Panther Cub PSURC1	East Lancs B41D	Warrington Corporation	92	R

Notes:
LHT 911   Rebodied 1958 with 1950 body

Lancastrian Transport Trust

Contact address: 1 Beverley Grove, South Shore, Blackpool,
Lancashire FY4 2BG
E-mail: phlilip@higgs.freeserve.co.uk
Brief description: The trust is dedicated to preserving historic buses
from Lancashire. Vehicles can often be seen at local rallies and other
events.

Registration	Date	Chassis	Body	New to	Fleet No	Status
CCK 663	1949	Leyland Titan PD2/3	Brush L27/26R	Ribble Motor Services	2687	A
DFV 146	1949	Leyland Titan PD2/5	Burlingham FH31/23C	Blackpool Corporation	246	A
561 TD	1962	Daimler Fleetline CRG6LX	Northern Counties H43/33F	Lancashire United Transport	97	R
RRN 405	1962	Leyland Atlantean PDR1/1	Weymann L38/33F	Ribble Motor Services	1805	R
YFR 351	1962	Leyland Titan PD3/1	Metro-Cammell FH41/32R	Blackpool Corporation	351	A
CTF 627B	1964	Leyland Titan PD2A/27	Massey H37/27F	Lytham St Annes Corporation	70	RP
HFR 512E	1967	Leyland Titan PD3A/1	Metro-Cammell H41/30R	Blackpool Corporation	512	R
PFR 554H	1970	AEC Swift MP2R	Marshall B47D	Blackpool Corporation	554	R
ATD 281J	1970	Leyland Atlantean PDR1A/1	Northern Counties H44/33F	Lytham St Annes Corporation	77	R
RTJ 422L	1972	Daimler Fleetline CRG6LXB-33	Northern Counties H47/32F	Lancashire United Transport	394	A

Notes:
CTF 627B   On loan from St Helens Transport Museum

Legionnaire Group

Contact address: 66 Montfort Road, Strood, Rochester, Kent
ME2 3EX
E-mail: bob.wingrove@btinternet.com
Brief description: The group aims to restore at least one of each
combination of chassis/Legionnaire so that Harrington's last body
style is represented in preservation.

Registration	Date	Chassis	Body	New to	Fleet No	Status
72 MMJ	1964	Bedford VAL14	Harrington C52F	Reliance Coaches, Meppershall	72	RP
CDK 409C	1965	Bedford VAL14	Harrington C52F	Yelloway Motor Services, Rochdale		A
JNK 681C	1965	Ford Thames 36 676E	Harrington C52F	Capital Coaches, London		RP

Notes:
JNK 681C   Used as Harrington demonstrator when new

Above right: The oldest surviving Daimler Fleetline is Northern Counties-bodied 561 TD, new as Lancashire United 97 in 1962, and now preserved by the Lancastrian Transport Trust. This evocative picture was taken at Salford's Greengate terminus. *Philip Lamb*

Right: The Lancastrian Transport Trust owns a number of former Blackpool vehicles, including 1967 Leyland PD3/MCW 512 (HFR 512E) and 1970 AEC Swift/Marshall 554 (PFR 554H). *Philip Lamb*

Meltham Mills Bus Museum

Contact address: 1 Vicar Park Road, Norton Tower, Halifax
HX2 ONL
Brief description: A collection of privately-owned vehicles most of
which operated originally in West Yorkshire.

Events planned: Please see enthusiast press for details.
Opening days/times: The collection is not normally open to the
public, but an appointment to view can be arranged by contacting the
above address.

Registration	Date	Chassis	Body	New to	Fleet No	Status
JUB 29	1928	Leyland Titan TD2	Eastern Counties L27/26R	Keighley-West Yorkshire Joint Services	K451	A
JX 7046	1939	AEC Regent O661	Park Royal H30/26R	Halifax Corporation	80	A
JX 9106	1946	AEC Regal O662	Weymann	Hebble Motor Services	181	A
AJX 369	1946	AEC Regent III 9612E	Park Royal H33/26R	Halifax Joint Omnibus Committee	243	A
HHP 755	1948	Maudslay Regal III 9621E	Duple FC33F	Greenslades Tours, Exeter		A
JXN 370	1949	Leyland Titan PD2/1 ('7RT')	Park Royal H30/26RD	London Transport	RTL47	A
BCP 671	1950	AEC Regent III 9612E	Park Royal H33/26R	Halifax Joint Omnibus Committee	277	R
LTF 254	1950	AEC Regent III 9612E	Park Royal H33/26R	Morecambe & Heysham Corporation	69	R
ROD 765	1958	AEC Regent V MD3RV	Metro-Cammell H33/26RD	Devon General Omnibus & Touring Co	DR765	R
3916 UB	1959	AEC Regent V 2D3RA	Metro-Cammell H38/32R	Leeds City Transport	916	R
LJX 215	1960	AEC Regent V 2D3RA	Metro-Cammell H40/32F	Halifax Joint Omnibus Committee	215	RP

Notes:

JUB 29	Rebodied in 1951 with 1932 body	HHP 755	Exhibited at 1948 Commercial Motor Show
JX 9106	Converted to tow lorry in 1956 and renumbered L4	JXN 370	Originally H30/26R

Below left: Most vehicles at the Meltham Mills Bus Museum are of AEC manufacture. The collection includes 1950 Park Royal-bodied Regent IIIs LTF 254, new as Morecambe & Heysham 69, and BCP 671, delivered to Halifax as 277, seen here in the company of a similar, but privately-owned, former Nottingham bus. *Stephen Morris*

Right: 1950 AEC Regent III/Park Royal BCP 671 was new to the Halifax Joint Omnibus Committee as No 277, and is seen participating in the 1998 Heart of the Pennines Rally. *Chris Dyson*

Below: Leeds City Transport also favoured AEC for its double-deckers, and was another operator to specify exposed radiators on Regent Vs. 1959 Metro-Cammell-bodied 916 (3916 UB) is shown re-enacting service 11 in September 1999. *Philip Lamb*

Merseyside Transport Trust

Contact address: 88 Hawthorne Road, Bootle, Merseyside, L20 9JX
E-mail: rob@aquaventurers.co.uk
Affiliation: NARTM; AEC Society; Leyland Society
Brief description: A collection of around 35 vehicles, mostly from the
Merseyside area but including others of special interest.

Registration	Date	Chassis	Body	New to	Fleet No	Status
GKD 434	1946	AEC Regent II O661	Weymann/LCPT H30/26R	Liverpool Corporation	A233	A
HKF 820	1949	AEC Regent III 9612E	Weymann/LCPT H30/26R	Liverpool Corporation	A344	RP
JKC 178	1949	Daimler CVA6	Northern Counties H30/26R	Liverpool Corporation	D553	A
KMN 519	1950	Leyland Comet CPO1	Park Royal B30F	Douglas Corporation	21	R
LFM 756	1951	Bristol LL6B	ECW B39R	Crosville Motor Services	SLB175	R
DWG 526	1951	Leyland Royal Tiger PSU1/15	Leyland C41C	W. Alexander & Sons	PC30	A
MMN 302	1951	Leyland Olympic HR40	Weymann B40F	Isle of Man Road Services	84	R
NMN 907	1952	Leyland Royal Tiger PSU1/13	Leyland B44F	Isle of Man Road Services	89	A
MKB 994	1952	AEC Regent III 9613A	Crossley H30/26R	Liverpool Corporation	A801	A
NKD 536	1953	AEC Regent III 9613S	Crossley H30/26R	Liverpool Corporation	A36	RP
NKD 540	1954	AEC Regent III 9613S	Saunders-Roe H32/26R	Liverpool Corporation	A40	RP
RKC 262	1955	Leyland Titan PD2/20	Alexander H32/26R	Liverpool Corporation	L161	RP
SKB 168	1956	Leyland Royal Tiger PSU1/13	Crossley/LCT RC44F	Liverpool Corporation	XL171	RP
SKB 224	1956	Leyland Titan PD2/20	Crossley H32/26R	Liverpool Corporation	L227	RP
JCK 542	1956	Leyland Titan PD2/12	Burlingham H33/28RD	Ribble Motor Services	1467	A
VKB 711	1956	Leyland Titan PD2/20	Crossley H33/29R	Liverpool Corporation	L255	RP
VKB 841	1957	Leyland Titan PD2/20	Crossley H33/29R	Liverpool Corporation	L320	A
VKB 900	1957	AEC Regent V D3RV	Metro-Cammell H33/29R	Liverpool Corporation	A267	R
KCK 869	1958	Leyland Titan PD3/4	Burlingham FH41/31F	Ribble Motor Services	1523	A
116 TMD	1958	AEC Bridgemaster B3RA	Park Royal H45/31R	ACV Sales		A
371 BKA	1959	AEC Regent V LD2RA	Park Royal FH40/32F	Liverpool Corporation	E1	R
372 BKA	1959	Leyland Atlantean PDR1/1	Metro-Cammell H44/34F	Liverpool Corporation	E2	RP
256 SFM	1961	Bristol Lodekka FLF6B	ECW H38/22F	Crosville Motor Services	DFB43	A
875 VFM	1962	Bristol Lodekka FSF6G	ECW H34/26F	Crosville Motor Services	DFG65	RP
891 VFM	1962	Bristol Lodekka FSF6G	ECW O34/26F	Crosville Motor Services	DFG81	RP
501 KD	1962	Leyland Atlantean PDR1/1	Metro-Cammell H43/35F	Liverpool Corporation	L501	R
67 UMN	1964	Leyland Titan PD3A/1	Metro-Cammell H41/32R	Isle of Man Road Services	60	R
GFM 180C	1965	Bristol Lodekka FS6B	ECW H33/27RD	Crosville Motor Services	DFB180	RP
FKF 801D	1966	Leyland Atlantean PDR1/1	MCW H43/35F	Liverpool City Transport	L801	A
FKF 835E	1967	Leyland Atlantean PDR1/1	MCW H43/28D	Liverpool City Transport	L835	RP
FKF 933G	1968	Leyland Panther PSUR1A/1R	MCW B47D	Liverpool City Transport	1054	RP
SKB 695G	1969	Bristol RELL6G	Park Royal B45D	Liverpool City Transport	2025	RP
UKA 562H	1969	Leyland Atlantean PDR2/1	Alexander H47/32D	Liverpool City Transport	1111	R
XKC 862K	1971	Leyland Atlantean PDR2/1	Alexander H49/31D	Merseyside PTE	1235	R
BKC 236K	1972	Leyland Atlantean PDR1A/1Sp	Alexander H43/32F	Merseyside PTE	1236	RP
JWM 689P	1976	Leyland Atlantean AN68/1R	East Lancs H43/32F	Merseyside PTE	1689	R

Notes:

SKB 168	Originally B40D, numbered SL171; rebuilt by Metro-Cammell in 1961	67 UMN	Originally registerd 7 MAN; re-registered and renumbered 67 in 1970
116 TMD	Former AEC demonstrator; acquired by Liverpool Corporation (EB) in 1959	GFM 180C	Now fitted with Gardner 6LW engine
891 VFM	Originally H34/26F		

Right: Numerically Liverpool's first long-wheelbase Leyland Atlantean/Alexander, 1111 (UKA 562H) did not enter service until after the formation of Merseyside PTE. Now cared for by the Merseyside Transport Trust, it is pictured in Croxteth. *Terry Morris*

Mike Sutcliffe Collection

Phone: Phone/Fax: 01525 221676
Affiliation: NARTM; Leyland Society member
Brief description: A collection of 20 vehicles, mainly buses of Leyland manufacture from the period 1908 to 1934, this is the largest collection of solid-tyred buses in the world, including the oldest British-built motorbus.

Opening days/times: Viewing can be arranged by prior appointment only. There is no charge, but donations are welcome.

Registration	Date	Chassis	Body	New to	Fleet No	Status
LN 7270	1908	Leyland X2	Tilling O18/16RO	London Central Motor Omnibus Co	14	R
LF 9967	1913	Leyland S3.30.T	Birch O20/16RO	Wellingborough Motor Omnibus Co	H	R
HE 12	1913	Leyland S3.30.T	Brush B27F	Barnsley & District Electric Traction Co	5	RP
CC 1087	1914	Leyland S4.36.T3	Leyland Ch32	London & North Western Railway	59	R
BD 209	1921	Leyland G7	Dodson Ch32D	United Counties Omnibus Co	B15	R
C 2367	1921	Leyland G2	Phoenix O23/20RO	Todmorden Joint Omnibus Committee	14	R
DM 2583	1923	Leyland SG7	Leyland FB40D	Brookes Bros ('White Rose'), Rhyl	27	RP
XU 7498	1924	Leyland LB5	Dodson O26/22RO	Chocolate Express Omnibus Co	B6	R
BT 8939	1925	Leyland C7	Barnaby B26R	Lee & Beulah, Elloughton	17	RP
PW 8605	1926	ADC 415	United B35F	United Automobile Services	E64	A
VF 8157	1930	Chevrolet LQ	Bush & Twiddy C14D	Final, Hockwold		R
CK 4518	1931	Leyland Lion LT2	Leyland B30F	Ribble Motor Services	1161	A
YG 7831	1934	Leyland Tiger TS6	Northern Counties	Todmorden Joint Omnibus Committee	15	A

Notes:

LF 9967	On loan to British Commercial Vehicle Museum, Leyland	C 2367	On loan to Manchester Museum of Transport
CC 1087	Re-registered XA8086 in 1919; reverted to CC 1087 in 1980	VF 8157	Originally registered VF 9126; acquired by Mulleys Motorways, Ixworth, in 1940
		YG 7831	Rebuilt as recovery vehicle; to be restored as bus

Left: Chocolate Express was one of the many 'pirate' operators to challenge London General's monopoly in the 1920s. The former's 1924 Leyland LB5/Dodson No B6 (XU 7498) survives in the Mike Sutcliffe Collection, which includes a number of early Leylands painstakingly restored using hand-built mechanical components.
Philip Lamb

North East Bus Preservation Society

Contact address: 'Relly Steading', Broom Park, Durham DH7 7RJ
Phone: 0191 384 5146
E-mail: r.l.kell@Durham.ac.uk
Affiliation: NARTM
Brief description: The collection is displayed at an 1820 former

locomotive shed on the Bowes Railway. This accommodates up to 10 vehicles, and so vehicles rotate between this and other locations. If you wish to view a particular vehicle, you will need to mention this when making arrangements to view.

Opening days/times: Viewing by prior arrangement only.

Registration	Date	Chassis	Body	New to	Fleet No	Status
CN 4740	1931	SOS IM4	Short B34F	Northern General Transport Co	540	A
CN 6100	1934	Northern General Transport SE6	Short B44F	Northern General Transport Co	604	RP
BTN 113	1934	Daimler COS4	Northern Coachbuilders B34R	Newcastle Corporation	173	A
DPT 848	1939	Leyland Tiger TS8	Roe B32F	Sunderland District Omnibus Co	159	R
EF 7380	1942	Leyland Titan TD7	Roe H26/22C	West Hartlepool Corporation	36	R
HHN 202	1947	Bristol L5G	ECW B35R	Bell's Services, Westerhope		R
HUP 236	1947	Albion Valiant CX39N	Associated Coachbuilders C33F	Economic Bus Services, Whitburn	W7	R
JPT 544	1948	Daimler CVD6	Willowbrook B35F	Venture Transport Co, Consett	156	R
LVK 123	1948	Leyland Titan PD2/1	Leyland H30/26R	Newcastle Corporation	123	RP
CFK 340	1948	AEC Regal III 6821A	Burlingham C33F	H. & E. Burnham, Worcester		R
ABR 433	1949	Crossley DD42/7C	Crossley H—/—R	Sunderland Corporation	100	RP
NVK 341	1950	AEC Regent III 9613A	Northern Coachbuilders H30/26R	Newcastle Corporation	341	R
LPT 328	1950	AEC Regal III 9621E	Burlingham C33F	Gillet Bros, Quarrington Hill	31	R
CBR 539	1952	Guy Arab III	Roe H33/25R	Sunderland Corporation	139	RP

Above: Co Durham independent operator Gillett Bros, of Quarrington Hill, was taken over by United in 1974. The firm's memory is perpetuated by LPT 328, a 1950 AEC Regal III/ Burlingham coach, now part of the North East Bus Preservation Society's collection, and seen at the 1999 Metro Centre rally in Gateshead. *David Reed*

Registration	Date	Chassis	Body	New to	Fleet No	Status
PHN 699	1952	Guy Arab III	Roe B41C	Darlington Corporation	26	RP
SHN 301	1953	AEC Regal IV 9821E	Burlingham C41C	Scotts Greys, Darlington	5	R
DCN 83	1954	Beadle-AEC	Beadle C35F	Northern General Transport Co	1483	A
SPT 65	1955	Guy Arab LUF	Weymann B44F	Northern General Transport Co	1665	RP
TUP 859	1956	AEC Regent V MD3RV	Roe H35/28R	Hartlepool Corporation	4	RP
UFJ 292	1957	Guy Arab IV	Massey H30/26R	Exeter Corporation	52	R
VUP 328	1957	Leyland Tiger Cub PSUC1/1	Crossley B44F	Economic Bus Services, Whitburn	A2	A
MJD 759	1958	AEC Reliance MU3RV	Roe C41C	Essex County Coaches, Stratford		R
YPT 796	1958	AEC Reliance MU3RV	Roe C41C	Economic Bus Services, Whitburn	W3	R
AFT 930	1958	Leyland Titan PD3/4	Metro-Cammell H41/32R	Tynemouth & District Omnibus Co	230	RP
WNL 259A	1962	AEC Reliance 4MU3RV	Plaxton B55F	Economic Bus Services, Whitburn	W5	R
221 JVK	1962	Leyland Atlantean PDR1/1	Alexander H44/34F	Newcastle Corporation	221	RP
6249 UP	1963	Leyland Leopard PSU3/3RT	Alexander DP51F	Venture Transport Co, Consett	249	R
ACU 304B	1964	Leyland Leopard PSU3/3R	Plaxton B55F	Stanhope Motor Services		R
PCN 762	1964	AEC Routemaster 3R2RH	Park Royal H41/31F	Northern General Transport Co	2099	R
EUP 405B	1964	AEC Routemaster 3R2RH	Park Royal H41/31F	Northern General Transport Co	2105	R
WBR 248	1964	Atkinson Alpha PM746HL	Marshall B45D	Sunderland Corporation	48	R
FBR 53D	1966	Leyland Panther PSUR1/1R	Strachans B47D	Sunderland Corporation	53	R
ECU 201E	1967	Bristol RESL6L	ECW B45D	South Shields Corporation	1	R
WHN 411G	1969	Bristol VRTSL6LX	ECW H39/31F	United Automobile Services	601	A
PCW 203J	1971	Bristol RESL6L	Pennine B45F	Burnley, Colne & Nelson Joint Transport Committee	103	R
MCN 30K	1972	Leyland/NGT Tynesider	Weymann/NGT H39/29F	Northern General Transport Co	3000	R
GGR 103N	1974	Leyland Atlantean AN68/2R	Northern Counties H47/36F	OK Motor Services, Bishop Auckland		RP
GUP 907N	1975	Bristol LH6L	ECW B43F	United Automobile Services	1623	R
TUP 329R	1976	Bristol VRTSL3/501	ECW H43/31F	Northern General Transport Co	3329	RP
RCU 838S	1977	Leyland Fleetline FE30AGR	Alexander H44/30F	Tyne & Wear PTE	838	R

Notes:

HHN 202	Rebodied 1957 with 1946 body; passed to Durham District Sevices (DB216) in 1959	PCN 762	Originally registered RCN 699
ABR 433	Fitted with Gardner 5LW engine	MCN 30K	Rebuilt from 1958 Leyland Titan PD3/4 new to Tyneside Tramways & Tramroads Co (49)
WNL 259A	Originally registered 8031 PT		registered NNL 49
ACU 304B	Originally registered 6 MPT	RCU 838S	Originally H44/27D

Left: Bristol RESL/ECW ECU 201E was new in 1967 as South Shields No 1; it is currently restored in its later guise as Tyne & Wear 341, and is seen in Gateshead in 1999. *David Reed*

Ribble Vehicle Preservation Trust

Contact address: 6 Crompton Road, Lostock, Bolton BL6 4LP
Brief description: The Trust promotes the preservation and restoration of vehicles from Ribble and associated companies.

Registration	Date	Chassis	Body	New to	Fleet No	Status
RN 7588	1935	Leyland Tiger TS7	Burlingham B35F	Ribble Motor Services	209	R
ACK 796	1944	Guy Arab II	Northern Counties/Bond L27/26R	Ribble Motor Services	2413	A
CRG 811	1947	Daimler CVD6	Alexander C35F	Aberdeen Corporation	11	A
CRS 834	1948	Daimler CVD6	Walker/Aberdeen CT C31F	Aberdeen Corporation	44	A
CCK 359	1948	Leyland Titan PD2/3	Leyland L27/26R	Ribble Motor Services	2584	A
MTC 540	1950	AEC Regent III 9613E	Park Royal H30/26R	Morecambe & Heysham Corporation	72	RP
DRN 289	1950	Leyland Titan PD2/3	Leyland L27/26RD	Ribble Motor Services	1349	A
DCK 219	1951	Leyland Titan PD2/3	East Lancs FCL27/22RD	Ribble Motor Services	1248	RP
SPU 985	1951	Leyland Olympic HR44	Weymann DP40F	Jennings Coaches, Ashen		A
ECK 934	1952	Leyland Titan PD2/12	Leyland L27/26RD	Ribble Motor Services	1364	A
ERN 700	1952	Leyland Royal Tiger PSU1/13	Leyland B8FI	Ribble Motor Services	377	R
FCK 884	1954	Leyland Tiger Cub PSUC1/1T	Saunders-Roe B44F	Ribble Motor Services	452	R
HRN 39	1955	Leyland Titan PD2/13	Metro-Cammell H33/28RD	Ribble Motor Services	1399	A
JCK 530	1956	Leyland Titan PD2/12	Burlingham H33/28RD	Ribble Motor Services	1455	R
JRN 41	1956	Leyland Tiger Cub PSUC1/2T	Burlingham C41F	Ribble Motor Services	975	RP
881 BTF	1957	Leyland Titan PD2/41	East Lancs H35/28R	Lancaster City Transport	881	A
528 CTF	1957	Leyland Titan PD2/40	Weymann L29/28RD	J. Fishwick & Sons, Leyland	5	R
KCK 914	1958	Leyland Titan PD3/4	Burlingham FH41/31F	Ribble Motor Services	1553	A
NRN 586	1960	Leyland Atlantean PDR1/1	Metro-Cammell H44/33F	Ribble Motor Services	1686	R

Above: Many former Ribble vehicles are now in the care of the Ribble Vehicle Preservation Trust. One such is 452 (FCK 884), a 1954 Leyland Tiger Cub bodied by Saunders-Roe. *David Reed*

Registration	Date	Chassis	Body	New to	Fleet No	Status
SFV 421	1960	Leyland Atlantean PDR1/1	Weymann CH34/16Ft	W. C. Standerwick	25	A
PRN 145	1961	Leyland Atlantean PDR1/1	Metro-Cammell H44/33F	Scout Motor Services, Preston	5	RP
PRN 906	1961	Leyland Titan PD3/4	Metro-Cammell H39/31F	Preston Corporation	14	RP
TCK 465	1963	Leyland Leopard PSU3/1R	Marshall B53F	Ribble Motor Services	465	RP
ARN 811C	1965	Leyland Leopard PSU3/3RT	Weymann DP49F	Ribble Motor Services	811	RP
TAO 179G	1969	Bedford SB5	Duple C41F	Hamilton's Coaches, Workington		R
HRN 249G	1969	Bristol RELL6G	ECW B41D	Ribble Motor Services	249	RP
FPT 6G	1969	Leyland Leopard PSU3/3RT	Plaxton C51F	Weardale Motor Services, Frosterley		A
NCK 338J	1971	Bristol RESL6L	ECW B47F	Ribble Motor Services	338	RP
OCK 350K	1971	Bristol RESL6L	ECW B47F	Ribble Motor Services	350	A
PRN 79K	1972	Bristol VRLLH6L	ECW CH42/18Ct	W. C. Standerwick	79	RP
NNC 855P	1976	AEC Reliance 6U3ZR	Duple C49F	Yelloway Motor Services, Rochdale		R
MFR 306P	1976	Leyland Leopard PSU3C/2R	Alexander B53F	Lancaster City Transport	306	R

Notes:

RN 7588	Rebodied 1949	ERN 700	Originally B44F
CRG 811	Rebodied 1958	SFV 421	'Gay Hostess' double-deck motorway coach
CRS 834	Body rebuilt 1962	TAO 179G	On display at British Commercial Vehicle Museum, Leyland
DCK 219	'White Lady' double-deck coach		

Left: Independent operator J. Fishwick & Sons is based in Leyland, and favoured the town's bus manufacturer until the end of production. 528 CTF was Fishwick's No 5, and is a 1957 Leyland PD2 with lowbridge Weymann bodywork. *Philip Lamb*

Right: SELNEC was the name of the Passenger Transport Executive formed in 1969 to assume control of municipal fleets in **S**outh **E**ast **L**ancashire and **N**orth **E**ast **C**heshire. It soon devised its own 'Standard' double-deck design; 7206 (VNB 177L), a Northern Counties-bodied Daimler Fleetline of 1972, is one of the few dual-door Standards built, and is now owned by the SELNEC Preservation Society.

On the left of the picture is the Chesterfield 123 Group's eponymous 1973 Daimler Fleetline/Roe, NNU 123M. *Stephen Morris*

SELNEC Preservation Society

Contact address: 16 Thurleigh Road, Didsbury, Manchester M20 2DF

Brief description: A collection of buses from the SELNEC era including SELNEC Standards, the trail-blazing 'Mancunian' and other vehicles from the Greater Manchester area.

Events planned: The operational vehicles will appear at a range of local rallies and shows.

Registration	Date	Chassis	Body	New to	Fleet No	Status
EN 9965	1950	Leyland Titan PD2/4	Weymann	Bury Corporation	165	RP
DNF 708C	1965	Daimler Fleetline CRG6LX	Metro-Cammell O43/29F	Manchester Corporation	4708	A
END 832D	1966	Leyland Atlantean PDR1/2	MCW H43/32F	Manchester Corporation	3832	RP
LNA 166G	1968	Leyland Atlantean PDR2/1	Park Royal H20/08D	Manchester City Transport	1066	R
NNB 547H	1969	Leyland Atlantean PDR2/1	East Lancs H47/32F	Manchester City Transport	1142	A
NNB 589H	1970	Daimler Fleetline CRG6LXB	Park Royal H47/28D	SELNEC PTE	2130	A
ONF 865H	1970	Leyland Atlantean PDR2/1	Park Royal H47/28D	SELNEC PTE	1177	A
RNA 220J	1971	Daimler Fleetline CRG6LXB	Park Royal H47/29D	SELNEC PTE	2220	A
PNF 941J	1971	Leyland Atlantean PDR1A/1	Northern Counties H43/32F	SELNEC PTE	EX1	R
TNB 759K	1972	Daimler Fleetline CRG6LXB	Northern Counties H45/27D	SELNEC PTE	EX19	A
VNB 177L	1972	Daimler Fleetline CRG6LXB	Northern Counties H45/27D	SELNEC PTE	7206	R
YDB 453L	1972	Seddon Pennine IV-236	Seddon DP25F	SELNEC PTE	1700	RP
WWH 43L	1973	Daimler Fleetline CRG6LXB	Park Royal H43/32F	SELNEC PTE	7185	R
XJA 534L	1973	Leyland Atlantean AN68/1R	Park Royal H43/32F	SELNEC PTE	7143	A
AJA 408L	1973	Bristol VRTSL6LX	ECW H43/32F	SELNEC Cheshire Bus Co	408	RP
XVU 341M	1973	Seddon Pennine IV-236	Seddon B23F	SELNEC PTE	1711	A
XVU 363M	1974	Seddon Pennine IV-236	Seddon B19F	Greater Manchester PTE	1733	A
BNE 729N	1974	Seddon Pennine IV-236	Seddon B19F	Greater Manchester PTE	1735	A
BNE 751N	1974	Leyland Atlantean AN68/1R	Northern Counties H43/32F	Greater Manchester PTE	7501	A

Registration	Date	Chassis	Body		New to	Fleet No	Status
BNE 764N	1974	Bristol LH6L	ECW B43F		Greater Manchester PTE	1321	A
OBN 502R	1977	Leyland Fleetline FE30AGR	Northern Counties H43/32F	Lancashire United Transport	485	A
XBU 1S	1978	Leyland Fleetline FE30AGR	Northern Counties H43/32F	Greater Manchester PTE	8001	RP
BNC 960T	1979	Leyland Atlantean AN68A/1R	Park Royal H43/32F		Greater Manchester PTE	7960	A
GBU 1V	1979	MCW Metrobus DR101/6	MCW H43/30F		Greater Manchester PTE	5001	RP
GNF 15V	1980	Leyland Titan TNTL11/1RF	Park Royal H47/26F		Greater Manchester PTE	4015	A
DWH 706W	1980	Leyland Fleetline FE30AGR	Northern Counties H43/32F	Lancashire United Transport	613	R
C751 YBA	1985	Dennis Domino SDA 1201	Northern Counties B24F		Greater Manchester PTE	1751	RP

Notes:

EN 9965	Converted to breakdown vehicle	VNB 177L	Exhibited at 1972 Commercial Motor Show
DNF 708C	Originally H43/29F; awaiting repatriated from USA	OBN 502R	Passed to Greater Manchester PTE (6901) in 1981
LNA 166G	Originally H47/29D; converted by Greater Manchester	C751 YBA	Exhibited at 1984 Commercial Motor Show
	PTE for use as 'Exhibus' exhibition vehicle — restored in this condition	DWH 706W	Passed to Greater Manchester PTE (6990) in 1981
PNF 941J	Exhibited at 1970 Commercial Motor Show as prototype SELNEC Standard		

Right: The Seddon Pennine RU was never a common type, and few survive in preservation. BCR 379K was new as Southampton 15 in 1972, and is now in the care of the Solent Transport Trust. *Philip Lamb*

Solent Transport Trust

Contact address: 'Paynter', Hook Lane, Hook-by-Warsash, Southampton SO31 9HH
Affiliation: NARTM; WOMP

Brief description: The collection includes a selection of Southampton's fleet from the early 1970s. The small membership carries out restoration work.

Registration	Date	Chassis	Body	New to	Fleet No	Status
JOW 928	1956	Guy Arab UF	Park Royal B39F	Southampton Corporation	255	A
318 AOW	1962	AEC Regent V 2D3RA	Park Royal H37/29R	Southampton Corporation	318	A
335 AOW	1963	Leyland Titan PD2A/27	Park Royal H37/29R	Southampton Corporation	335	A
BTR 361B	1964	AEC Regent V 2D3RA	Neepsend H37/29R	Southampton Corporation	361	R
JOW 499E	1967	AEC Swift MP2R	Strachans B47D	Southampton Corporation	1	A
KOW 910F	1967	AEC Regent V 3D2RA	Neepsend H40/30R	Southampton Corporation	402	A
PCG 888G	1968	AEC Reliance 6U3ZR	Plaxton C55F	Coliseum Coaches, Southampton		A
PCG 889G	1968	AEC Reliance 6MU3R	Plaxton C45F	Coliseum Coaches, Southampton		A
TTA 400H	1970	Bedford SB5	Duple C41F	Otter Coaches, Ottery St Mary		A
BCR 379K	1972	Seddon Pennine RU	Seddon B44F	Southampton Corporation	15	R

Notes:

JOW 928	Originally B36D
BTR 361B	On display at CPPTD Museum, Portsmouth
PCG 888G	Originally C57F

Three Counties Bus Museum

Contact address: 18 Greenriggs, Hedley Park, Stopsley, Luton
LU2 9TQ
Phone: 01525 370578 or 01582 413200
E-mail: tcbm@lodekka.demon.co.uk
Affiliation: NARTM; BBPG; CVPG
Brief description: Established to provide a focus for bus preservation
in Bedfordshire, Buckinghamshire and Hertfordshire. Seeks to ensure
a long-term future for the vehicles and secure permanent undercover
accommodation.
Events planned: Please see enthusiast press for planned Operating
Days.

Registration	Date	Chassis	Body	New to	Fleet No	Status
BXD 628	1935	Leyland Cub KPO3	Short B20F	London Transport	C4	RP
FXT 122	1939	Leyland Cub REC	LPTB B20F	London Transport	CR16	RP
LYR 915	1952	AEC Regent III O961	Weymann H30/26R	London Transport	RT3496	R
MLL 555	1952	AEC Regal IV 9821LT	Metro-Cammell B37F	London Transport	RF168	R
MXX 317	1953	Guy Special NLLVP	ECW B26F	London Transport	GS17	R
MXX 332	1953	Guy Special NLLVP	ECW B26F	London Transport	GS32	R
MXX 434	1953	AEC Regal IV 9821LT	Metro-Cammell B39F	London Transport	RF457	R
NLE 527	1953	AEC Regal IV 9821LT	Metro-Cammell B38F	London Transport	RF308	R
NLE 627	1953	AEC Regal IV 9821LT	Metro-Cammell B39F	London Transport	RF627	R
BNH 246C	1965	Daimler CVG6	Roe H33/26R	Northampton Corporation	246	R
KBD 712D	1966	Bristol Lodekka FS6G	ECW H33/27RD	United Counties Omnibus Co	712	R
DEK 3D	1966	Leyland Titan PD2/37	Massey H37/27F	Wigan Corporation	140	R
UXD 129G	1968	Bristol RELL6L	ECW B48D	Luton Corporation	129	RP
NPD 127L	1973	Leyland National 1151/1R/0402	Leyland National B49F	London Country Bus Services	LNC27	A
SOA 674S	1977	Leyland Leopard PSU3E/4R	Plaxton C49F	Midland Red Omnibus Co	674	R

Above left: London Transport's RF class of Metro-Cammell-bodied AEC Regal IVs numbered 700 buses, many of which survive in preservation. The Three Counties Bus Museum has four, including RF457 (MXX 434) of 1953.

Left: Also part of the Three Counties collection is former United Counties 712 (KBD 712D), an ECW-bodied Bristol FS new in 1966. *Philip Lamb*

Westgate Museum

Contact address: Enquiries: 14 Ilkley Road, Caversham, Reading
RG4 7BD
Brief description: The collection, near Doncaster, is housed in a
former Methodist Chapel built in 1865. The vehicles operate at
Sandtoft Transport Centre from time to time.
Opening days/times: Viewing strictly by appointment.

Registration	Date	Chassis	Body	New to	Fleet No	Status
RC 8472+	1944	Sunbeam W	Weymann H30/26R	Derby Corporation	172	R
SVS 281	1945	Daimler CWA6	Duple H30/26R	Douglas Corporation	52	R
DRD 130+	1949	BUT 9611T	Park Royal H33/26RD	Reading Corporation	144	R
LDP 945	1956	AEC Regent III 6812A	Park Royal L31/26RD	Reading Corporation	98	R
WLT 529	1960	AEC Routemaster R2RH	Park Royal H36/28R	London Transport	RM529	R
+ Trolleybus						

Notes:
SVS 281   Originally registered FMN 955.

West Midlands Bus Preservation Society

Contact address: 36 Victoria Road, Bradmore, Wolverhampton WV3 7EU

Brief description: The main core of the collection is of vehicles from the West Midlands PTE in the period 1969 to 1986. Other artefacts are being collected for inclusion in a planned transport museum.

Opening days/times: Vehicles can be viewed by special arrangement.

Registration	Date	Chassis	Body	New to	Fleet No	Status
GKE 68	1939	Bristol K5G	Weymann H28/26R	Chatham & District Traction Co	874	A
DUK 278	1946	Guy Arab II	Roe H31/25R	Wolverhampton Corporation	378	RP
KHA 301	1948	BMMO C1	Duple C30C	BMMO ('Midland Red')	3301	R
GOU 732	1949	Tilling-Stevens K6MA7	Scottish Aviation C33F	Altonian Coaches, Alton		R
LTA 813	1950	Bristol KS5G	ECW L27/28R	Western National Omnibus Co	994	R
OTT 43	1953	Bristol LS6G	ECW C39F	Western National Omnibus Co (Royal Blue)	2200	R
UHY 362	1955	Bristol KSW6B	ECW H32/28R	Bristol Tramways & Carriage Co	C8233	R
56 GUO	1961	Bristol MW6G	ECW C39F	Western National Omnibus Co (Royal Blue)	2267	RP
KOV 436	1964	Daimler Fleetline CRG6LX	Park Royal H44/33F	Birmingham City Transport	3436	A
AEH 143C	1965	AEC Reliance 2MU4RA	Plaxton C41F	Potteries Motor Traction Co	C1043	A
ARN 658C	1965	Leyland Titan PD3A/1	Metro-Cammell H39/31F	Preston Corporation	73	A
EHA 424D	1966	BMMO D9	BMMO/Willowbrook H40/32RD	BMMO ('Midland Red')	5424	RP
OTA 640G	1969	Bristol RELH6G	ECW C45F	Southern National Omnibus Co (Royal Blue)	2380	R
NOV 880G	1969	Daimler Fleetline CRG6LX	Park Royal H43/29D	Birmingham City Transport	3880	RP
SOE 913H	1969	Daimler Fleetline CRG6LX-33	Park Royal H47/33D	West Midlands PTE	3913	A
TOB 997H	1970	Daimler Fleetline CRG6LX-33	Park Royal H47/33D	West Midlands PTE	3997	RP
YOX 133K	1971	Daimler Fleetline CRG6LX	Park Royal H43/33F	West Midlands PTE	4133	RP
CKC 304L	1972	Daimler Fleetline CRG6LXB	MCW H43/32F	Merseyside PTE	3004	A
NOB 413M	1974	Bristol VRTSL6LX	MCW H43/33F	West Midlands PTE	4413	A
NOC 600R	1976	Leyland Fleetline FE30AGR	Park Royal H43/33F	West Midlands PTE	6600	A
SDA 757S	1977	Leyland Fleetline FE30AGR	East Lancs H43/33F	West Midlands PTE	6757	A
WDA 835T	1978	MCW Metrobus DR102/1	MCW H43/30F	West Midlands PTE	6835	RP
WDA 956T	1978	Leyland Fleetline FE30AGR	MCW/WMT B37F	West Midlands PTE	1956	A
WDA 986T	1978	Leyland Fleetline FE30AGR	MCW H43/33F	West Midlands PTE	6986	R

Notes:

DUK 278	Rebodied 1952
ARN 658C	No staircase — converted to driver training vehicle by West Midlands PTE (8658)
TOB 997H	Gardner 6LXB engine fitted after acquisition by C. J. Partridge & Son, Hadleigh
WDA 835T	Exhibited at 1978 Commercial Motor Show
WDA 956T	Originally double-deck bus (H43/33F) 6956; rebuilt as single-decker in 1994

Right: GOU 732 is a 1949 Tilling-Stevens K6 with Scottish Aviation coach bodywork, new to Altonian Coaches. Now housed by the West Midlands Bus Preservation Society, it carries 'Wulfrun' names appropriate to its new home, along with a green and yellow livery reminiscent of Wolverhampton Corporation.
David Reed

Below: Birmingham and its successors operated Daimler-designed buses for 93 years. Former West Midlands 1978 Leyland Fleetline/MCW 6986 (WDA 986T) was one of the last to remain in service in 1997, and has now been restored to original condition.
Philip Lamb

West of England Transport Collection

Contact address: 15 Land Park, Chulmleigh, Devon, EX18 7BH
Affiliation: NARTM
Brief description: A large private collection of vehicles, mainly from West Country major operators. The collection includes buses, coaches and transport memorabilia.

Events planned: 1 October 2000 — Annual WETC Open Day
Opening days/times: Viewing at other times by prior arrangement.

Registration	Date	Chassis	Body	New to	Fleet No	Status
UO 2331	1927	Austin 5PL	Tiverton B13F	Sidmouth Motor Co		RP
VW 203	1927	Leyland Lion PLSC3	Mumford B—R	National Omnibus & Transport Co	2407	A
JY 124	1932	Tilling-Stevens B10A2 Express	Beadle B—R	Western National Omnibus Co		A
OD 5868	1933	Leyland Lion LT5	Weymann B31F	Devon General Omnibus & Touring Co	68	A
OD 7497	1934	AEC Regent I O661	Short O31/24R	Devon General Omnibus & Touring Co	DR210	A
OD 7500	1934	AEC Regent I O661	Brush H30/26R	Devon General Omnibus & Touring Co	DR213	R
ADV 128	1935	Bristol JO5G	Beadle B—R	Western National Omnibus Co		A
ATT 922	1935	Bristol JJW6A	Beadle B35R	Western National Omnibus Co		RP
AUO 74	1935	Leyland Lion LT5A	(chassis only)	Devon General Omnibus & Touring Co	SL79	A
AAX 27	1935	Leyland Bull TSC9	(chassis only)	West Monmouthshire Omnibus Board	13	A
BTF 25	1936	Leyland Titan TD4c	Leyland FH30/24R	Lytham St Annes Corporation	45	A
ETT 995	1938	AEC Regal I rebuild	Saunders-Roe H30/26R	Devon General Omnibus & Board	DR705	A
BOW 169	1938	Bristol L5G	-	Hants & Dorset Motor Services	TS676	A
EUF 204	1938	Leyland Titan TD5	Park Royal H28/26R	Southdown Motor Services	204	A
EFJ 241	1938	Leyland Titan TD5	Leyland H30/26R	Exeter Corporation	26	A
EFJ 666	1938	Leyland Tiger TS8	Cravens B32R	Exeter Corporation	66	R
DOD 474	1940	AEC Regal I O662	Weymann B35F	Devon General Omnibus & Touring Co	SR474	A
FTA 634	1941	Bristol K5G	ECW L27/28R	Western National Omnibus Co	345	RP
GTA 395	1942	Bristol LL5G	BBW B39R	Southern National Omnibus Co	373	RP
JTA 314	1943	Guy Arab II	Roe H31/25RD	Devon General Omnibus & Touring Co	DG314	A
DJY 965	1948	Crossley DD42/5	Crossley L27/26R	Plymouth Corporation	335	RP
GLJ 957	1948	Leyland Titan PD1A	ECW L27/26R	Hants & Dorset Motor Services	PD959	A
MAF 544	1949	Austin CXB	Mann Egerton C31C	J. J. Pollard, Hayle		RP
KUO 972	1949	Bristol K6B	ECW L27/28R	Western National Omnibus Co	959	A
JFJ 606	1949	Daimler CVD6	Brush H30/26R	Exeter Corporation	43	A
HJY 296	1953	Leyland Titan PD2/12	Leyland H30/26R	Plymouth Corporation	396	A
TFJ 808	1956	Guy Arab IV	Massey H30/26R	Exeter Corporation	50	A
OCO 502	1958	Leyland Titan PD2/40	Metro-Cammell H30/26R	Plymouth Corporation	102	R
974 AFJ	1960	Guy Arab IV	Massey H31/26R	Exeter Corporation	74	R
1 RDV	1964	AEC Reliance 2MU3RA	Harrington C41F	Devon General Omnibus & Touring Co (Grey Cars)	1	R
CTT 513C	1965	AEC Regent V 2D3RA	Park Royal H40/29F	Devon General Omnibus & Touring Co	513	R
GNM 235N	1975	Bristol LHL6L	Plaxton C51F	Cobholm Hire Service ('Caroline-Seagull'), Great Yarmouth		R
CRM 927T	1979	Leyland-DAB	Leyland AB64T	South Yorkshire PTE	2006	A
C748 FFJ	1985	Ford Transit 190D	Carlyle B16F	Devon General	748	R

Notes:

UO 2331	Body new 1933
VW 203	Body new 1936
JY 124	New body and engine fitted in 1947
OD 7497	Converted to open-top in 1955
OD 7500	Rebodied 1949
ADV 128	Rebodied 1950
ATT 922	Rebodied in late 1940s
AUO 74	Front end of chassis only
ETT 995	Rebuilt in 1953 using prewar mechanical components and rebodied
BOW 169	New with Beadle body; acquired by Wilts & Dorset Motor Services (504) in 1952 and converted to breakdown vehicle in 1956
EUF 204	Rebodied 1949
EFJ 241	Converted to tree-cutter in 1958
EFJ 666	Used as a snow plough 1952-6
FTA 634	Damaged in 1941 by enemy action and rebuilt
GTA 395	Lengthened and rebodied in 1954
CTT 513C	Restored by the Oxford Bus Museum Trust
CRM 927T	Articulated prototype (57ft long)

Above: Plaxton-bodied Bristol LHL GNM 235N was new to Caroline-Seagull Coaches of Great Yarmouth in 1975. It now forms part of the West of England Transport Collection at Winkleigh. *Paul Chancellor*

These two Leyland double-deckers, owned by the Lancastrian Transport Trust, hail from neighbouring municipal fleets. Former Blackpool 512 (HFR 512E) is an MCW-bodied PD3 of 1967, while former Lytham St Annes 77 is a Northern Counties-bodied Atlantean of 1970. *Philip Lamb*

Indices

Index of Vehicles by Registration Number

123

SS 7501	70	UDT 455F	68	VRD 193	68	XHA 482	24
SSC 212P	74	UF 1517	19	VRF 372	28	XHA 496	24
SSX 602V	74	UF 6473	19	VRU 124J	88	XHO 370	84
STO 523H	58	UF 6805	19	VSC 86	72	XJA 534L	111
SUK 3	24	UF 7428	19	VTU 76	43	XKC 862K	104
SVS 281	115	UFC 430K	60	VUD 30X	61	XLG 477	43
SVS 904	43	UFJ 292	108	VUP 328	108	XM 7399	48
SWS 671	72	UFM 52F	81	VV 5696	93	XMS 252R	74
SWS 715	72	UHA 255	24	VV 9135	70	XON 41J	21
SYG 561	43	UHA 956H	24	VVF 543	93	XRU 277K	88
		UHA 963H	24	VVP 911	24	XSL 945A	72
TAO 179G	110	UHA 969H	21	VW 203	118	XSN 25A	72
TBC 164	18	UHA 981H	25	VY 957	52	XTC 684	27
TBK 190K	30	UHJ 842	28	VZI 44	78	XTF 98D	64
TCH 274L	25	UHY 359	90	VZL 179	78	XU 7498	106
TCK 465	110	UHY 362	116			XVC 290	21
TDH 914	68	UHY 384	90	W 963	58	XVU 341M	111
TDJ 612	64	UI 8511	78	WBR 246	99	XVU 352M	53
TDK 322	75	UKA 562H	104	WBR 248	108	XVU 363M	111
TDL 126S	41	UKE 830X	61	WCG 104	97	XVX 19	28
TDL 567K	94	UL 1771	27	WDA 700T	21	XWX 795	68
TDL 998	41	UMA 370	52	WDA 835T	116	XX 9591	32
TE 5110	78	UMP 227	32	WDA 956T	116		
TE 5780	98	UO 2331	118	WDA 986T	116	YDB 453L	111
TE 7870	84	UOU 417H	97	WDF 569	24	YDK 590	52
TE 8318	46	UOU 419H	97	WEX 685M	94	YDL 318	41
TET 135	75	UP 551	57	WFM 801K	44	YDW 756K	97
TF 6860	43	UTC 672	52	WFN 513	34	YFR 351	100
TF 818	46	UTU 596J	24	WG 3260	70	YG 7831	106
TFJ 808	118	UU 6646	32	WG 8107	70	YHT 958	90
TGM 214J	73	UUA 214	43	WG 8790	70	YLG 717F	43
THL 261H	94	UWA 296L	75	WG 9180	75	YLJ 147	88
THM 692M	81	UXD 129G	116	WH 1553	46	YLJ 286	36
TJ 836	84			WHL 970	94	YNX 478	60
TJO 56K	60	VBA 151S	64	WHN 411G	108	YOX 133K	116
TMS 585H	73	VD 3433	70	WLT 371	72	YPT 796	108
TNA 496	52	VDL 264K	41	WLT 506	21	YR 3844	48
TNA 520	52	VDV 760	75	WLT 529	115	YRC 194	58
TNB 759K	111	VF 2788	39	WLT 991	64	YRT 898H	36
TOB 997H	116	VF 8157	106	WNG 864H	25	YSD 350L	73
TOE 527N	25	VFU 864J	73	WNL 259A	108	YSG 101	72
TRJ 109	64	VH 2088	98	WNO 478	28	YTE 826	36
TRJ 112	52	VH 6188	88	WRA 12	75	YWL 134K	60
TRN 731	43	VH 6217	88	WT 7108	57	YYJ 914	72
TTA 400H	113	VJO 201X	61	WT 9156	98	YYS 174	72
TTD 386H	52	VK 5401	57	WTE 155D	64		
TUO 497	93	VKB 711	104	WUS 248	72	ZC 714	78
TUP 329R	108	VKB 841	104	WV 1209	39	ZD 7163	78
TUP 859	108	VKB 900	104	WW 4688	92	ZD 726	80
TV 9333	67	VL 1263	46	WWH 43L	111	ZH 3926	78
TWH 809K	86	VLT 108	58	WWJ 754M	68	ZH 3937	78
TWL 928	60	VLT 140	56	WYJ 813	34	ZH 4538	78
TWS 910T	90	VM 4439	51	WZJ 724	78	ZI 9708	78
TWT 123	94	VMP 10G	72			ZJ 5933	78
TWW 766F	43	VMP 8G	72	XAK 355L	44	ZL 2718	78
TWY 8	94	VNB 101L	53	XBU 1S	112	ZL 6816	78
TXJ 507K	53	VNB 177L	111	XC 8059	48	ZO 6819	78
TY 9608	94	VO 6806	56	XDH 516G	24	ZO 6857	78
TYD 888	72	VO 8846	58	XDH 56G	24	ZO 6881	78
		VR 5742	52	XDH 72	92	ZO 6949	78
UCS 659	72	VRC 612Y	58	XFM 42G	73	ZU 9241	78
UCX 275	72	VRD 186	36	XG 9304	70	ZY 79	78

A booklet of indices of chassis type, body and operator is available from NARTM, PO Box 5141, Burton-upon-Trent DE15 0ZF, priced £2.99

Index of Museums and Collections